Everest
the Cruel Way

Everest
the Cruel Way

Climbing Mount Everest at its hardest: the 1980 winter attempt on the infamous west ridge

JOE TASKER

Vertebrate Publishing, Sheffield
www.v-publishing.co.uk

Everest the Cruel Way

Joe Tasker

Vertebrate Publishing
Crescent House, 228 Psalter Lane, Sheffield S11 8UT, United Kingdom
www.v-publishing.co.uk

First published in Great Britain in 1981 by Methuen (London).
This edition first published in 2016 by Vertebrate Publishing.

This book is a work of non-fiction based on the life, experiences and recollections
of Joe Tasker. In some limited cases the names of people, places, dates and sequences
or the detail of events have been changed solely to protect the privacy of others.

A CIP catalogue record for this book is available from the British Library.

ISBN 978-1-911342-23-6 (Paperback)
ISBN 978-1-906148-74-4 (Ebook)

Produced by Vertebrate Publishing.
Printed and bound by Lightning Source.

Contents

Foreword: A Great Partnership

by Chris Bonington

It was 15 May 1982 at Advance Base on the north side of Everest. It's a bleak place. The tents were pitched on a moraine the debris of an expedition in its end stage scattered over the rocks. Pete and Joe fussed around with final preparations, packing their rucksacks and putting in a few last minute luxuries. Then suddenly they were ready, crampons on, rope tied, set to go. I think we were all trying to underplay the moment.

'See you in a few days.'

'We'll call you tonight at six.'

They set off, plodding up the ice slope beyond the camp through flurries of wind-driven snow. Two days later, in the fading light of a cold dusk, Adrian Gordon and I were watching their progress high on the North East Ridge through our telescope. Two tiny figures on the crest outlined against the golden sky of the late evening, moving painfully slowly, one at a time. Was it because of the difficulty or the extreme altitude, for they must have been at approximately, 27,000 feet (8230 metres)?

Gradually they disappeared from sight behind the jagged tooth of the Second Pinnacle. They never appeared again, although Peter's body was discovered by members of a Russian/Japanese expedition in the spring of 1992, just beyond where we had last seen them. It was as if he had lain down in the snow, gone to sleep and never woken. We shall probably never know just what happened in those days around 17 May, but in that final push to complete the unclimbed section of the North East Ridge of Everest, we lost two very special friends and a unique climbing partnership whose breadth of talent went far beyond mountaineering. Their ability as writers is amply demonstrated in their books.

My initial encounter with Peter was in 1975 when I was recruiting for the expedition to the South West Face of Everest. I was impressed by his maturity at the age of 23, yet this was combined with a real sense of fun and a touch of 'the little boy lost' manner, which he could use with devastating effect to get his own way. In addition, he was both physically and intellectually talented. He was a very strong natural climber and behind that diffident, easy-going manner had a personal drive and unwavering sense of purpose. He also had a love of the mountains and the ability to express it in writing. He was the youngest member of the Everest team and went to the top with our Sherpa sirdar, Pertemba, making the second complete ascent of the previously unclimbed South West Face.

As National Officer of the BMC, he proved a diplomat and a good committee man. After Dougal Haston's death in an avalanche in Switzerland, he took over Dougal's International School of Mountaineering in Leysin. He went on to climb the sheer West Face of Changabang with Joe Tasker, which was the start of their climbing partnership. It was a remarkable achievement, in stark contrast to the huge expedition we had had on Everest. On Changabang there had just been Pete and Joe. They had planned to climb it alpine-style, bivouacking in hammocks on the face, but it had been too cold, too great a strain at altitude, and they had resorted to siege tactics. Yet even this demanded huge reserves of determination and endurance. The climb, in 1976, was probably technically the hardest that had been completed in the Himalaya at that time, and Pete describes their struggles in his first book, *The Shining Mountain*, which won the John Llewelyn Rhys Prize in 1979.

Pete packed a wealth of varied climbing next few years. In 1978 both he and Joe joined me on K2. We attempted the West Ridge but abandoned it comparatively low down after Nick Estcourt was killed in an avalanche. In early 1979 Pete reached the summit of the Carstensz Pyramid, in New Guinea, with his future wife, Hilary, just before going to Kangchenjunga (the world's third highest mountain) with Joe, and Doug Scott and Georges Bettembourg That same autumn he led a small and comparatively another team on a very bold ascent of the South Summit of Gauri Sankar.

The following year he returned to K2 with Joe, Doug and Dick Renshaw. They first attempted the West Ridge, the route that we had tried in 1978, but abandoned this a couple of hundred metres higher than our previous high point. Doug Scott returned home but the other three made two very determined assaults on the Abruzzi Spur, getting to within 600 metres of the summit before being avalanched off on their first effort, and beaten by bad weather on a subsequent foray. Two years later Pete and Joe, with Alan Rouse, joined me on Kongur, at the time the third-highest unclimbed peak in the world. It proved a long drawn out, exacting expedition.

Joe Tasker was very different to Peter, both in appearance and personality. This perhaps contributed to the strength of their partnership. While Pete appeared to be easy going and relaxed, Joe was very much more intense, even abrasive. He came from a large Roman Catholic family on Teesside and went to a seminary at the age of 13 to train for the priesthood, but at the age of 18 he had begun to have serious doubts about his vocation and went to study sociology at Manchester University. Inevitably, his period at the seminary left its mark. Joe had a built-in reserve that was difficult to penetrate but, at the same time, he had an analytical, questioning mind. He rarely accepted an easy answer and kept going at a point until satisfied that it had been answered in full.

In their climbing relationship had a jokey yet competitive tension in which neither of them being wished to be the first to admit weakness or to suggest retreat. It was a trait that not only contributed to their drive but could also cause them to push themselves to the limit.

Joe had served an impressive alpine apprenticeship in the early 'seventies when, with Dick Renshaw, they worked through some of the hardest climbs in the Alps, both in summer and winter. These included the first British ascent (one of the very few ever ascents) of the formidable and very remote East Face of the Grandes Jorasses. In addition they made the first British winter ascent of the North Wall of the Eiger. With Renshaw he went on to climb, in alpine-style, the South Ridge of Dunagiri. It was a bold ascent by any standards, outstandingly so for a first Himalayan expedition. Dick was badly frostbitten and this led to Joe inviting Pete to join him on Changabang the start of their climbing partnership.

On our K2 expedition in 1978, I had barely had the chance to get to know Joe well, but I remember bring exasperated by his constant questioning of decisions, particularly while we were organising the expedition. At the time I felt he was a real barrack-room lawyer but, on reflection, realised that he probably found my approach equally exasperating. We climbed together throughout the 1981 Kongur expedition and I came to know him much better, to find that under that tough outer shell there was a very warm heart. Prior to that, in the winter of 1980-81, he went to Everest with a strong British expedition to attempt the West Ridge. He told the story in his first book, *Everest the Cruel Way*.

Our 1982 expedition to Everest's North East Ridge was a huge challenge but our team was one of the happiest and most closely united of any trip I have been on. There were only six in the party and just four of us, Joe, Pete, Dick Renshaw and I, were planning to tackle the route. Charlie Clarke and Adrian Gordon were there in support going no further than Advance Base. However, there was a sense of shared values, affection and respect, that grew stronger through adversity, as we came to realise just how vast was the undertaking our small team was committed to.

It remained through those harsh anxious days of growing awareness of disaster, after Pete and Joe went out of sight behind the Second Pinnacle, to our final acceptance that there was no longer any hope.

Yet when Pete and Joe set out for that final push on 17 May I had every confidence that they would cross the Pinnacles and reach the upper part of the North Ridge of Everest, even if they were unable to continue to the top. Their deaths, quite apart from the deep feeling of bereavement at the loss of good friends, also gives that sense of frustration because they still had so much to offer in their development, both in mountaineering and creative terms.

Chris Bonington
Caldbeck
September 1994

to give a reply – Brian was getting a lift to the Lake District with Chris, who was in a hurry. I had a sensation of giddiness as the beauty of the idea, the breathtaking audacity of such a suggestion, hit me and at the same time a rapid vision of all the impossibilities – work involvements, lack of money, lack of time, personal relationships – the traditional dilemma of the climber, the conflict between his career, social life, love life, security and the fulfillment which comes from the all-absorbing commitment to some heady project. I gave Brian a quick 'yes' and agreed to speak with him later. A few days later I received from Chamonix a letter from Alan Rouse with details of their plans and a typed list, with my name and address already on it, of the eight members of the expedition. My consent had been taken for granted; asking was simply a formality!

The winter of 1981/82 seemed suitably far off, almost two-and-a-half years away, and I could comfortably shelve the idea until nearer the time. In the last eighteen months I had been away on three expeditions – nine months in total, hardly leaving myself time to unpack from one trip before re-packing for the next. My shop was being run on a chaotic basis, the days just not being long enough for all that there was to do, and I relied heavily upon the invaluable work of the shop's manager, Alf. There had already been one casualty in my private life as a result of my absence abroad, when I came back from the second expedition in six months, with a six-week period at home between the two trips, to find that my girlfriend had decided she had had enough of associating with someone whom she only saw every few months.

I was returning to K2 in the spring of 1980 and after that I planned to spend some time at home to concentrate on work and generally getting my affairs into some sort of order. A longish spell at home seemed very desirable, with even the possibility of finding the leisure to do some rock climbing which expeditions preclude. At the end of that spell was the enthralling prospect of Everest in winter, which I had not focused on clearly but which in the back of my mind I knew was the next logical step for me.

Some months after I was first invited we learnt that the winter period of 1981/82 was not available to us, making our options 1980/81 or some date five years hence. Suddenly the leisured approach to Everest vanished – a hard decision had to be made. The later date was hardly worth considering, for by then the route may well have been climbed, taking away some of the unknown element. The 1980/81 date, less than twelve months away, was a little too close and we would be hard pressed to raise the money and organize the equipment for then. For my part I was already committed to an expedition to K2 which, all being well, I would only be back from three months before going away again. Life was going a little too fast. It seemed clear that 1980/81 was the only sensible choice and, faced with a decision, I realized that it was all-important for me to go on the Everest winter expedition because it promised to be extremely hard, and improbable, the finest challenge in the sport that I could conceive of. It was so obviously the next logical step forward in mountaineering, to climb in the Himalayas in winter, that I felt the idea had been part of my consciousness for years. Come what may, I decided to go.

The team was to be made up of a small group of friends, most of whom had climbed together for a number of years. The birth of the original, daring idea was due to Alan Rouse and Brian Hall, who had taken part in a bold, lightweight ascent of the 25,300-foot Jannu in eastern Nepal. Both Alan and Brian had climbed all over the world with first ascents and impressive repeats to their credit, particularly in South America where they had spent many months. They had used their worldwide experience to start a guiding service which had the whole world as its territory.

Alan, in the early 1970s, had been representative of a volatile new generation of rock climbers. Whilst still in his early teens, endowed with a fine natural ability which was belied by his studious air of abstraction, he was instrumental in setting a new trend in climbing with the boldness of some of his ascents. Unusually for someone who excelled in one facet of the sport, he began to transfer his attention to the bigger mountains, disclosing a drive and imagination beneath the deliberately cultivated exterior of a person dedicated to enjoyment and anarchy. He seemed a complex character, able to engage in the most serious of discussions and gain the respect of people from all walks of life, yet sometimes finding himself inexplicably involved in the most outrageous of escapades. Whatever he embarked upon, he wanted to go to the limit with it. He had studied mathematics at Cambridge and one sometimes got the impression that he tolerated, good naturedly, conversations on any subject but that his mind was flying along at a rapid pace and that he could assimilate concepts and spit out answers with the speed of a computer. Attacking Everest in winter was an astonishing idea but it was typical of Alan's cheek that he should have come up with it.

For a number of years, Brian and Alan had been close friends, Brian providing a sound, organizational sense to counterbalance Alan's prolific ideas. There was a contradiction in Brian in that he had acquired a reputation for outlandish, wild behaviour but when he turned his attention to organizing such a thing as an expedition, he displayed unsuspected responsibility and a forceful persuasiveness which ensured that his side of a job was always completed.

Alan and Brian had climbed in South America with the Burgess twins, Adrian and Alan, two of the climbing world's most colourful characters. Identical twins, tall, broad and blond, of Viking descent, seeming to have inherited their forebears' predilection for rape and pillage, they are known as strong and resourceful mountaineers, specializing in survival. Alan Rouse used to say of them that they were the best people he had ever met as companions on a mountain. They were an automatic choice.

Paul Nunn is a prominent figure in mountaineering, not least for his infectious laugh which accompanies each tale from his vast repertoire of anecdotes and tall stories. Paul has been an established figure in climbing since many of us could remember. There is a restless energy about Paul which sends him off every year to some part of the world on a filming, if not a climbing, assignment, and the same restlessness, the same determination not to miss anything that might happen, keeps him up till all hours of the night to be the last one to leave a pub or party. He has an endless capacity for conversing on any topic imaginable and, a wry scepticism about life in general. Paul, without being overweight, is a solid bulk. His massive hands wrapped round a mug of beer seem to demonstrate a strength of personality as well as of physique. His experience over many years covers most of Europe, the Pamirs, The Caucasus, the Karakorum and the Indian Himalayas. As a lecturer in Economic History, he has a respectability that many of us lacked, and Alan asked him along on account of his solid background as a mountaineer as well as his potential for raising sponsorship from local firms to whom he was well known.

Pete Thexton was asked to come as the doctor, but his unpublicized record of achievement in the Himalayan regions of Kulu and Garwhal hinted at a quiet determination and hidden strength. Physically Pete appeared small, but he was stocky and strong. He is one of those people who change in appearance each time one looks at them, leaving the impression that they have been totally underestimated. He was least known of all the team to any of the members but on paper, at least, if there was going to be anyone as doctor, Pete was as well qualified as any doctor we knew to appreciate the medical problems of high altitude and also take part in the expedition as a full climbing member. To an ambitious climber, though, the added burden of ministering to the sick was a potentially frustrating responsibility.

John Porter, half-American, half-English, lives in an out-of-the-way town on the west side of the Lake District. One of the mystery men of the climbing scene, appearing periodically to go off on an expedition, usually with Polish climbers, and achieving a high reputation for his persistence and ability, he had climbed in the Hindu Kush, in India, and. South America.

If Alan Rouse was of a scientific temperament, John was of an artistic one, with all that that entails of vague dreaminess, and the ability to reproduce the apt quotation. He always has a puzzled air and the resigned acceptance of a person who does not capitalize on his opportunities because he is too preoccupied with more abstract thoughts to be concerned with the practicalities of life.

I had not climbed with any of the members of the team, except for a rock route in North Wales once with Brian, but I lived close to most of them and saw them frequently on social occasions. I can only presume from this that in selecting a team, Alan and Brian felt that I would be able to integrate successfully with everyone else.

Expeditions can be so arduous, the members living in such close proximity to each other, that it is vital to have a group of people who are able to get on with: each other and work together. It is not essential that the team be made up of close friends; friendship and the ability to work together do not necessarily coincide. The bond which is formed by members of an expedition who have worked and struggled together goes beyond friendship, it is more akin to the relationship with a brother whom one knows intimately and accepts for all his faults as well as his good points and virtues.

I was interested at the prospect of forging the strong bonds of new friendship with seven people whom I knew and liked, and whose achievements I admired, but cautious too at the potential for discord that was contained in an enterprise which would throw us all together, for a long spell, under the most trying conditions.

1980 was a hectic year. We were faced with the problem of amassing the equipment and money for the winter expedition a full twelve months sooner than we had expected. Had it been another pre- or post-monsoon expedition it would not have been so much of a problem. The winter in the Himalayas, however, was a largely unexplored period for climbing and, from what little information we could gather, conditions would be much more unforgiving than at any other time of year. Our preparations would have to be rigorous and our equipment, as far as we could ensure, faultless.

The history of winter climbing in the Himalayas is very brief. The arrival of winter was generally felt to mark the end of the climbing season, as with the British attempt on the South-West Face of Everest in 1972. After nearly two months of continual effort, by the middle of November the lead climbers were moving to establish their top camp close to the rock band. On reaching the site for Camp 6, it was impossible to pitch a tent in the prevailing wind and climbing on the Rock Band above was also out of the question. Dougal Haston looked round the corner of the buttress onto what had been regarded as an escape route, an easier option of reaching the summit, to find that in such wind there were no easy options. Without his oxygen mask he felt that he would not have been able to breathe.

They had gone to their limit and, although success had eluded them, they had the inner satisfaction of knowing that it was through no weakness on their part that they had not made it. This was the start of winter, and as John Hunt was to say of the expedition later, 'No one who has experienced the appalling conditions prevailing at high altitude in the Himalayan winter can doubt that Bonington's team stopped in their tracks at the ultimate limit of human achievement imposed for the time being, by natural forces.'

In winter the 'jet-stream', the high winds which blow at anything up to 130 knots, usually at altitudes of around 35,000 feet, drop to lower altitudes, taking in the upper reaches of the Himalayan peaks. Little is known about wind behaviour on the mountains in winter but the widest-held belief was that above 25,000 feet a mountain was taking the full force of the jet-stream, and severe disturbance due to turbulence would be felt below that.

It was into this jet stream that Haston, Scott, MacInnes and Burke climbed on that November day in 1972, and against which they realized it was impossible to make any progress. Meanwhile, emphasizing the contrasts of winter, Jimmy Roberts was sitting on the hillside of Kalipatar at 19,000 feet, watching the lead climbers through binoculars. Comfortable under a hot sun in a clear sky, he could not understand the reasons for the retreat. He could only see the tiny figures moving up or down; he could not tell that the temperature was perhaps -30 degrees Celsius to -40 degrees Celsius, nor that the wind was gusting at 100 miles per hour. The coming winter was a deceptive time of extremes.

Polish climbers, somehow setting their own standards outside the mainstream of the climbing world, were the ones who applied themselves directly to the problems of climbing in winter in the Himalayas. The performance of Polish climbers has long, given cause for astonishment. They seem to have an aptitude for choosing bold, dangerous climbs that are often completed under duress and against great hardship. It seems fitting that it was the Poles who were the first to step into this punishing arena with their winter ascent of Noshaq, a 24,580-foot peak in the Hindu Kush, during January/February 1973.

They were well prepared in some ways, and learnt much during the expedition. They experimented with ointments as protection against the cold; they described the winds as being of hurricane force and temperatures ranging between -25 degrees Celsius to -50 degrees Celsius at night. With tents ruined by the winds and themselves worn out with fighting against them, they had given up hope of succeeding when they were blessed with a spell of fine, calm weather and reached the summit on the night of 13 February.

Some members suffered from frostbite but the expedition was an outstanding success. Already, on the way home from that achievement, they started planning their next winter expedition for 1974/75, only this time to Lhotse, 27,923 feet, the fourth highest peak in the world.

There they met the same harrowing conditions as on Noshaq. Three members had to return to Kathmandu due to illness and their inability to recover in the hostile climate of Base Camp. The rest fought a two-month-long battle against the wind and cold, finally being driven back only a few hundred feet below the summit by the unheralded arrival of a vicious storm. Without oxygen masks, like Dougal Haston, they felt that they would not have been able to breathe in the wind-driven snow. Their permit for the mountain expired on 31 December and, although they had come prepared for a long siege lasting until March, they had to withdraw or risk a total ban on their climbing in Nepal for a number of years.

From these few sources of information on winter mountaineering we were able to cull only an overall impression of an extremely bleak and hostile environment where daily existence was totally concerned with survival, leaving little chance of relaxation. Success seemed improbable, and if achieved it would only be through extraordinary hardship and persistence.

For me, once the dream had taken possession there was no other way; for friends and climbing colleagues, from the security of their own, more sane, future plans, the West Ridge of Everest in winter was a gruelling fantasy for which they expressed pity rather than admiration.

Early in 1980 we heard that the same team of Polish climbers had succeeded in climbing the South Col route up Everest on 17 February. They had applied the knowledge gained on the two previous expeditions to Noshaq and Lhotse, taken oxygen to assist them against the dreadful cold and winds, and through persistence against the most severe storms, finally reached the top.

The South Col route is the way the mountain was originally climbed and the way it has been climbed most often since. Sometimes it is disparagingly called 'The Yak Route', indicating its lack of technical difficulty and illustrating the stories of some expeditions only reaching the summit because the members are pushed or pulled up the route by their Sherpas, in much the same manner as the Sherpas treat their Yaks, the local beasts of burden. However, in winter there is no easy way up Everest, or indeed up any mountain.

Once again the Poles were caught in the skeins of bureaucracy in that the permission to climb Everest only came through to them in December, so they were halfway through the winter before they reached Base Camp. The official definition of the winter season by the Nepalese Ministry of Tourism is from 1 December to 31 January. This left the Poles little time to complete their ascent. An extension was allowed to 15 February, and a further extension requested. A couple of extra days were allowed but not the full length of time desired. It was a fitting reward for their determination that the Poles reached the summit on the last day that they were allowed to climb upwards.

Due to the arbitrary definition of the 'winter season' there was some doubt cast upon their claim to have climbed Everest in winter, as the date on which the summit was reached officially fell outside the dates defining winter. Consequently, in official terms Everest was still unclimbed in winter.

Mountaineers have long grown accustomed to the rules governing expeditions to the Himalayas but it comes as a surprise to many people that to be allowed to attempt to climb a peak in any of the Himalayan countries one has to 'book' it, and pay a fee ranging from £50 to £60 for modest peaks of around 20,000 feet to approximately £1,000 for the giants of Everest or K2. This is only the first step towards the mountain. One has to agree to abide by all the rules governing behaviour during the expedition, whether it be not photographing strategic bridges or only climbing between the fixed dates of the season allotted.

To citizens of a country which has not been invaded for a thousand years, such sensitivity over border security is incomprehensible. To people who are accustomed to wandering over their own hills and those of neighbouring countries at will, charging a fee to climb a mountain seems ludicrous. The Himalayas, however, mark a natural frontier which spans some of the most sensitive borders in the world. Periodically, in times of confrontation, whole mountain areas are put out of bounds, and only gradually, as international relations ease, are foreigners allowed back into the mountain regions, and only then when hedged in by regulations and accompanied by a government-appointed officer.

We would, of course, think nothing of it if we heard the fee charged for booking Wembley Stadium. It might be objected that this took some building and the fee is therefore justified, but we also have natural resources which we are prepared to pay, for, whether it be underground caverns or stretches of wasteland and a ticket collector charging you for parking your car. The Himalayan countries are all poor countries who use the demand for one of their own natural resources as a means of raising revenue.

The prospect of making the first overall winter ascent of Everest was very appealing but there was no doubt in any of our minds that the Poles had done what they set out to do – they had climbed Everest at the worst time of the year, whatever arbitrary definition of season might be attached to it. For us there were enough unknowns about our own projected ascent not to feel that the Poles in any way exhausted our interest in the mountain. The West Ridge is the most difficult route yet achieved on the mountain. It had been climbed in its entirety only once before, by a large Yugoslav expedition, and we planned to climb it in winter and without oxygen, testing further the limits of the possible.

Our expectations of finding a suitable sponsor for the expedition were disappointed. We needed £15,000 in cash, a minute amount in comparison with most other expeditions to Everest, for which the cost more normally amounts to tens of thousands of pounds. The low cost of our expedition was due both to our reliance solely on our own efforts on the mountain, and to our intention to climb without supplementary oxygen equipment. The cost of oxygen equipment and the logistics involved in transporting it up the mountain add enormously to an expedition's budget. We would have Sherpas at Base Camp, a small group comprising Sirdar, cook, cook boy and mail runner. The Sirdar coordinates hiring and organization of porters. The cook and cook boy relieve the expedition members of the more mundane tasks in order that they can concentrate on the climbing. Although the cost of hiring and equipping this Base Camp staff, along with equipping and paying our Liaison Officer, can add as much as one third to the budget of a small expedition, this cost is small in comparison to that of kitting out a team of Sherpas to act as load-carriers on the mountain.

Everest in winter did not fail to excite everyone's imagination, but in a period of extreme economic decline few firms felt that they could justify supporting a sporting venture when they were operating on a short working week or laying off many of their workers.

Alan was occupied with the task of raising money, spending much of his time on the telephone or meeting possible sponsors. Our hopes were raised and dashed time after time.

In the midst of all the preparations, I left for the expedition to K2 with two members from the 1978 attempt, Pete Boardman and Doug Scott, and Dick Renshaw, partner for much of my early climbing activities. In a way I could not concentrate fully on Everest until K2, 'The Savage Mountain', was safely finished with. It was an expedition lasting three-and-a-half months, at the end of which I emerged emaciated and exhausted after a prolonged assault which culminated in three of us, a few hours away from the summit, being buried in the middle of the night in an avalanche. It was as near to death and resurrection as I have been. When the horror of burial and suffocation was over, we spent three days slipping closer and closer to exhaustion as we fought for survival during the descent from the mountain.

I felt as if I had been to the brink of the abyss and looked over the edge; I felt purged by the experience. Rather than being deterred by the ordeal, I realized more clearly than ever before that climbing mountains was what I wanted to do. The reasons are not easy to define; the closest I can come to explaining them is that it makes me the person I am; going to the absolute limit of one's capabilities in anything is always satisfying.

My interest in Everest was not diminished, I had simply kept it dormant whilst I concentrated on K2. During the return from Pakistan my attention gradually centred fully on what was to come. Pete taunted me with comments on my folly at planning to leave again so soon, less than three months after our return. He had been on two expeditions the previous year and found it almost too demanding on his time and energy. This year he was planning a trek in the Himalayas. It was going to seem strange going on an expedition without Pete. We had hardly known each other before our two-man expedition to Changabang in 1976 when we had spent forty days completely alone together. Miraculously, our mutual assessment of each other's capabilities had proved accurate, and when we came out of our wilderness after the forty days we had not only realized a fantastic dream but had found a bond of friendship which, without words, could enable either one of us to anticipate the other's thoughts and reactions. It was to be the basis for further mountain ventures together.

Pete was disappointed that he had not been asked to come with us for the winter expedition. He had already been to the top of Everest once in 1975 with the South-West Face expedition, and he said that he did not really want to go again, but he would have liked to have been asked.

For my part, in the absence of someone on our team that I knew well, I hoped that I would have the experience and maturity to accommodate to all the different personalities in situations of stress, without any of the abrasiveness which is sometimes inevitable in the process of getting to know a person's inner self.

Alan asked me to be co-leader in the U.K. with a view to raising sponsorship. Unlike the more traditional styles of expedition with a strict, authoritarian leadership structure, the expeditions we had all been involved with were organized on a much more democratic basis. If there was a leader, it was as if by rota. From the point of view of obtaining permission from the Nepalese government it was necessary to have the name of one person as leader; for contacting sponsors it is essential to have a leader or co-leader as spokesman. Amongst, ourselves we each regarded the task of every member as equally important. For my part, I was very relieved to be free of the burden of organizing the equipment, a job which requires a great deal of paperwork and time – time being my most scarce resource. In my role as fund-raiser I set out to investigate the possibilities of making a film of the expedition and also to contact the main media outlets to arrange news coverage.

Exploring the prospects of making a film offered a new, interesting departure. Allen Jewhurst is a close friend and a director of Chameleon Films, which specializes in making independent adventure films. After some casting around to get the feel of the idea, I asked him to go ahead with arrangements to bring a film crew with us. The initial hope of raising money in advance, by selling the rights to a television company, came to nothing, but if a successful film was made we stood a chance of recovering some of our money afterwards.

I had known Allen for a number of years and greatly enjoyed his company. He had had a flirtatious relationship with the climbing scene since 1976 when he and his partner, Chris Lister produced the film of the ascent of the Trango Tower. As a friend I was glad for him to come with us, but as a business man with his own company I had never quite understood him. He seemed to have some involvement with most aspects of the TV world, and if it was not him personally it was 'one o' me companies', as he was fond of saying in his broad London accent. The offices of Chameleon Films in Leeds seemed to be plush and elegant beyond the visible means of the company. Since I only ever visited his offices after dark, I was never sure if the whole operation was not somehow reminiscent of the film 'The Sting' in which the façade of a betting office is erected to defraud someone (albeit a crook himself), and that if I returned in daylight I would not find the premises under a totally different guise. In fact, the Chameleon offices are still very much there and the company has a reputation as a serious programme maker.

Allen was full of enthusiasm for the idea of making a film and he enlisted the services of Mike Shrimpton as cameraman and Graham Robinson for sound. Mike had done some rock climbing and had travelled to most places in the world on TV assignments. On meeting him I was impressed at his thoroughness and ready grasp and appreciation of points at issue. Graham was very quiet, had no experience at all of climbing, and a look of panic would cross his face when anyone asked him if he was really going to Everest.

From past experience I knew that the presence of amiable outsiders to the climbing team can help to prevent the pressures and tensions of expedition life from getting out of proportion, but it was a major worry that something might happen to one of the film crew, who inevitably would not have much experience of the mountains they would have to live in, in bitter conditions, for the best part of three months. It was worry for their own sakes and for the sake of the expedition as a whole which affected me, for if any one of them did have an accident it would seriously affect the morale of the rest of us. On the 1972 South-West Face expedition, Tony Tighe, who was there simply to lend a hand round Base Camp, was killed during the final days of the expedition when a serac in the ice-fall collapsed on top of him. During the Polish winter attempt on Lhotse, Stanislaw Latallo, one of their film crew, died from exposure and exhaustion. There is danger all the time to, and it is more likely strike if one's attention is focused on something other than the conditions on the mountains.

Given these reservations, everyone on the team was keen to cooperate in obtaining the material to make the best possible film. Having 'outsiders' along, especially ones who are recording your every move and word, can be a cause of conflict in itself and an incentive to reticence. We hoped, however, that by being closely involved in the filming ourselves it would be 'our' film, the film crew would be an integral part of the team, and we would, thus have the opportunity of making the best, most accurate and intimate film on mountaineering that had ever been made.

John Porter was occupied amassing the food we were going to take with us in what little time he had free whilst organizing the Kendal Mountaineering Film Festival. Pete Thexton was left to his own devices selecting and collecting all the medical equipment, pills and medicines he thought we would need. Paul Nunn was away on the Royal Geographical Society Karakorum Project for a while and on his return he lent a hand with negotiations over the film contract and provided a central gathering point for all the equipment, food and medicine in his house in Sheffield, where his patient wife watched her home being overtaken by the creeping monstrosity of the expedition. The Burgess twins, Al and. Ade, who had been absent in Canada during most of the preparations, were sentenced to drive around collecting and packing all the outstanding pieces of equipment which had not already arrived.

As the date of departure drew nearer, so the number of calls from the press, television and radio increased. Whenever I had to speak to them I found myself repeating, as if rehearsed, the same things; my mouth seemed to produce the words while my brain was preoccupied with a dozen other things. Talking about a climb before I had actually done it was something I had never felt easy about. There was an element of shyness due to the doubts I had about my own competence or ability to succeed on any particular climb. I preferred the attempt to be my own private affair, or something shared with my climbing partner, but in going to the Himalayas it becomes necessary to announce beforehand one's intentions in order to obtain permission from the government in question and also to raise the necessary finance. It was an uncomfortable feeling on the first expedition I was involved with to have to tell people a full year beforehand what our intentions were.

Everest still excites the public's imagination more than any other mountain and there is a fascination with the dangerous aspects of attempting to climb it. Without having set foot on, the mountain, the climber setting out for Everest can be the focus of the dangerously seductive attention of the media. He is a modern-day gladiator whose fascination is that he is stepping into an arena from which he knows there is a chance that he might not return. This knowledge may be something that he would rather cope with privately but the arena which draws him, and the particular arena of Everest which was drawing us, is a public one and we had to accept the consequences.

After an interview in which I had been open and sincere, but which was one of many interviews in which I had been open and sincere, I would feel empty and a little drained. The words and conversation had not penetrated to my inner being, I had given a 'performance', thus protecting the real self inside. It made me uneasy to participate in exciting the interest of the public climb which involved all eight of us pushing ourselves to the limit and courting death for a sustained period of time. I would have preferred to be reticent about the whole enterprise but, without being rude, this was not possible, and at least cooperation would mean that the media would have the facts right.

Alan had suggested that half of the team went out at the beginning of November with all the equipment and food. They would sort out the formalities, clear customs and start walking with all the baggage and porters. The rest of us would fly out two weeks later, taking a flight from Kathmandu on a small plane to Lukla, an airstrip part-way along the route of approach to Everest. The whole approach march can take up to eighteen days from leaving the road. Flying to Lukla would cut about ten days off the journey. Alan had felt that those of us who had been away once already that year probably needed a bit more time in Britain. As usual, things arise to fill the space available, and although the feeling, after all the equipment and food had gone with the first four on 3 November, was something like the calm after a storm, there were many loose ends to tie up.

I was relieved to be spared the full length of the walk-in. Usually it is a time for relaxing; most of the problems of organization have been solved, life becomes a very simple one of walking, resting and a gradual focusing of the concentration on the mountain ahead. The formalities in Kathmandu, however, and all the petty tasks of buying local food, equipping the cooks and Sherpas of the Base Camp staff, are very demanding, and I felt that the four of us who were going later had been given the softer option.

Somehow, though, I regretted not leaving with the first four. They would be involved with the expedition right from the start, they would be getting to know each other and growing together, a vital part in forming the strong bonds which would be essential for us in working together on the mountain.

As a complete surprise came a phone call from No. 10 Downing Street – an invitation to lunch with the Prime Minister and her guests, the King and Queen of Nepal. I treated the call as a joke, thinking that some friends must be pulling my leg. I rang the number I had been given and sure enough the call was answered with 'Hello, Prime Minister's office'. I was due to fly to Nepal the day before the lunch date, but after consulting the other members it was clear that nothing would be lost by my flying out two days later. I was intrigued to pass through that well-known doorway. Paul Nunn, Brian Hall and John Porter took the plane on Tuesday 18 November. I spent the remaining time in London making final arrangements with *The Observer*, to which we would be sending back news reports, and similarly with ITN. I had discussions with a publisher who was interested in the story of the expedition and from Pentax I picked up an enormous 6 x 7cm camera which they were loaning to us for the expedition.

On the Wednesday I was running down Whitehall, late for the luncheon appointment, and hurried through the security checks outside 10 Downing Street and in through the door. It was as if I had stepped into Dr Who's time-ship, the 'Tardis'; outside it is a small, old-fashioned police box, inside it is enormous, exceeding, in some scientific fantasy, all proportions of the external shell. We are familiar with the little door of No.10, with the policeman outside, resembling the entrance to a small terraced house. Inside, staircases lead up and down, passageways branch off in all directions; there are innumerable doors, antechambers, spacious gathering places and a large dining hall. I shook hands with Mrs Thatcher, who appeared and spoke exactly as on television. The King and Queen of Nepal seemed tolerant of the ritual introductions, a formality which they were having to repeat throughout their stay in Britain. With relief I recognized a familiar face, John Denson, the British Ambassador to Nepal, who had welcomed us back from our success on Kangchenjunga with a champagne toast at his embassy residence. The meal was conducted at a brisk pace, the whole procedure obviously orchestrated by a master of ceremonies to fit in with the Prime Minister's busy schedule. Politely but firmly the meal was brought to an end and there was an irresistible momentum to leave. I stepped out onto the street, saying goodbye to the Densons and promising to visit them in Kathmandu, and rushed off to complete the thousand remaining things I had to do before leaving.

3   Going to the Widow Maker

Three months after returning from the expedition to K2 I was at Heathrow airport again, ready for another departure. One of my sisters, Carmel, her fiancé, Andy, and my girlfriend, Maria, were there. It was a strange parting. I was frantically re-packing, trying to avoid excess baggage charges; there was a delay whilst some ticket confusion was cleared up in the queue in front of me, and when it was my turn the flight had closed and there was a chance I might not get on. I rushed from one desk to another guided by idiotic, mistaken directions. My single-minded pre-occupation with expeditions over the past months had been distressing to Maria, who felt very much incidental to my climbing plans. Now at the last moment there was no time to talk. I was at last checked in and we ran up the escalator before the final turn round for the goodbye, having hardly conversed for the hour we had been at the airport. Maria had a suddenly tearful and drained face – so much was left unsaid before I turned to go through the hole of an entrance as if to execution.

I do not feel lonely on an expedition, and I do not feel a dread of separation. An expedition is all-absorbing and fulfilling. I have known more loneliness in a city than on a remote mountain where I have been absolutely alone for a week, with not even the sight of another person. On a mountain I have an identity, a purpose and a place within the lives of other people. If there are times when one is physically alone it is not through any personal rejection, but because a vital role is being performed.

It was a relief to settle into my seat on the plane knowing that I was at last rejoining the mainstream of the expedition. For the last two weeks I had felt uncomfortably separated from the members of the expedition who had gone on ahead. There were innumerable things that I had not sorted out before leaving, many letters I would have to write from Kathmandu, but already the discord due to diverse, competing demands was beginning to fade away. By the time we reached Base Camp the whole pace of life would have slowed down and life itself become very simple.

On the flight from Delhi to Kathmandu I had a view of the snowy mountains we had come to climb. They seemed more snowy than in summer, but it was not white everywhere; at least we would not be on snow all through the approach march too.

I joined Paul, Brian and John in Kathmandu, that amiable city, which was but it had not been another dimension of experience; it was more of the same excruciatingly hard work. On Kangchenjunga three of us had spent a night in a snow cave at 26,000 feet, climbing the next day the 2,000 feet to the summit and descending, in the night, to the same snow cave. It had not been a fight against an unwilling spirit; inside I knew I wanted to continue, but like an old man whose mind is still active when his strength is failing, the question was whether my body could perform all the necessary movements to reach the summit before dark. Every half-dozen steps upwards left us panting, gasping in lungfuls of rarefied air. We had reached the summit one hour before dark, without hallucinations, without distorted perception or dizziness. The only indication that our brains were affected by the altitude was that we did press on to the summit, in the face of a rising storm, knowing that we would inevitably get benighted.

Next day I walked along with Al Burgess, only identifiable from his brother by the stubbly beard which gave him a mischievous appearance. We talked again of high altitude, K2 and Kangchenjunga. Al and Ade are quite different in, temperament, outlook and even in some ways in their appearance, but these differences are only noticeable as one gets to know them both better. Even then, after not seeing them for a while, it is easy to mistake one for the other. In talking to one or other of them I usually felt a certain air of uncanniness, as if each one knew already what had been discussed with the other. As I talked again of K2 and Kangchenjunga, I could not help feeling that Al already knew what I was going to say, and that he had possibly only forgotten that I had already said these things the day before.

There is such a sense of togetherness in their awareness of each other, their intimate knowledge of each other, that the twins give an impression of strength that any union of separate parts gives. The girlfriend of one of them said that it is disconcerting to have a close relationship as no woman will ever be as close to either of them as they are to each other.

In the few days of preparations in Kathmandu, Al had met a girl who had become quite fond of him. She was planning to come up to meet him after we had finished on the mountain. We were planning to get Ade to grow a beard and impersonate his twin brother, with us in collusion calling him Al, to see how long it would take her, if at all, to spot the trick.

We left the village of Pheriche, climbing steeply up a narrow valley, enclosed by snowy mountains. At a col we passed a row of cairns, which stand, ominous as tombstones, to the memory of the Frenchman and five Sherpas who were swept away by an avalanche in their attempt to climb the West Ridge of Everest in 1974.

Lobuje is the last inhabited place on the way up to Everest. It consists of a few Yak herders' dwellings which are now occupied on a more consistent basis, catering for the trekkers who make it this far. A saying which has come into use is, 'See Lobuje and die', a dictum arising from the dangers inherent in this trek. Lobuje is at approximately 14,000 feet and to the unwary or unfit the possibility of a fatal attack of high-altitude sickness is very real. A small hospital has been built by the Japanese at Pheriche, the last village on the trail, specifically to care for the visitors who become sick.

Each day now we were only walking for a few hours. It would have been possible, but unwise, to do more. The height gain between each stage was considerable and at this altitude it is the going up high too quickly which causes high-altitude sickness. In 1978 I had visited this area on the way to Nuptse, the third peak of the Everest massif, when one member of our team became critically ill at Lobuje. We carried him down to Pheriche 1,500 feet lower where he was cared for by a Sherpani girl. He recovered and subsequently married the girl. The story is legendary in this area, the fairytale fantasy of a rich stranger carrying off his true love having been given credence by this event.

Unlike the mountain folk of India and Pakistan, Sherpa society is delightfully open and relaxed. It was possible to laugh and joke with the womenfolk, something unheard of in Pakistan. A tea house at Lobuje was run by a Sherpa girl, fluent in English and French. We spent an evening sitting, with eyes smarting from woodsmoke, drinking chang and playfully flirting with the Sherpa girl and her friends. Everyone does much manual labour in this hill society, carrying heavy loads and tilling the fields. Even the women are very strong and any attempt at going further than their rules of decorum permitted was firmly rebuffed. They were fascinated by our two blond clones, the Burgess twins. Blond hair is unknown among the Sherpas, and this together with the twins' incredible size in comparison with the diminutive Nepalese people and their similarity made an obvious focus for the giggling attentions of the easy going Sherpanis.

The girl running the tea house knew Samji, the girl who had married my expedition companion.

'Samji my friend. You want to marry Sherpani like her?'

'In England we have "one night marriage", what about that?'

'One night no good, all night very good,' and she would relapse into ribald convulsions of laughter with her friends.

Gorak Shep was the last camping place before Base Camp. We pitched our tents on the sandy bed of a dried up lake. From the hill behind it is possible to see Everest and we took it in turns to wander up for the view. I waited till late in the afternoon to catch the sunset on the mountain and sat for a freezing hour, growing progressively more numb in the chill breeze, recording the exquisite change of colours – from pink to deep orange – on Everest and the hills around. There did not seem to be much wind this day, but now the mountain looked huge and I was numbed with cold on a lowly hillock watching the sun slip away from the summit 12,000 feet higher.

We had a bleak, windswept evening meal, raked by sand from the dried-up lake bed, with the food congealing on the plates before there was time to finish eating.

We reached Base Camp on 6 December, end of one mode of existence and start of another. The winter snows had not lingered.

Our tents had to be pitched on the icy desert of the lower Khumbu glacier. Rocks churned up by the imperceptibly moving river of ice littered the surface. We spent a whole day hacking platforms from the ice and pitching tents with rocks to which we tied. The guylines It was worth the effort to make each tent site comfortable as we expected to be there for many weeks.

To the north the camp was overlooked by the steep walls leading up to the Lho La, the lowest point on the West Ridge, and the complex slopes leading up to the West Shoulder, 6,000 feet above us. In 1978 I had seen an avalanche break away from the walls of ice guarding the Lho La, sweeping down in seconds and covering our camp, over a mile distant, with fine snow. Anything in its path would have been obliterated. I had thought then that any attempt to gain the Lho La was suicidal, but the Yugoslavs had found a cunning, though difficult, route up the rock buttresses to the left, avoiding most of the danger. We intended to follow this safer line.

4 Attacking the Ramparts

The weather was fine and clear but definitely chilly, even on the sunniest day. It was hard to relax for long, for the cold penetrated right to the core. Paul Nunn, Pete Thexton and Alan Burgess were sick with dysentery or some related illness. We had thought to escape such illness in the sterile atmosphere of winter but the watering place for our last camp at Gorak Shep had been a stagnant pool and we suspected this to be the cause of the trouble. Only during the daylight hours between 8.30 a.m. and 4.30 p.m., if the sun was out, was there any semblance of warmth; those who were ill had little encouragement for recovery from our chill surroundings. Paul steadfastly refused, Pete's panacea for dysentery-related illness, the much feared Flagyl, the effect of which was sometimes more debilitating than the illness for the three days of the dosage. Paul, having gathered on his travels much experience of strange illnesses, preferred to try to cure himself in his own way. Almost all of us had colds, snuffles and coughs.

Alan was preoccupied with the tedious task of paying off our porters, calculating the expedition's expenditure and ensuring that we had enough cash available in Nepalese rupees for all our expenses until returning to Kathmandu.

John Porter, having shelved his responsibility as food organizer during the confusion of the approach walk, now got down to the task of locating and making available the rations and the delicacies designed to make Base Camp life enjoyable.

Brian Hall continued his never-ending work of sorting out and distributing the equipment which he had worked so hard to design and amass specifically for this expedition. Everything had to be accounted for; if there was anything lost or forgotten there was little chance of replacing it before the end of the expedition.

Al and Ade Burgess and I were privileged to be free to make the first exploratory steps towards finding a safe route up the 2000 feet of rock to the Lho La.

It was only meant as a reconnaissance, we wanted to find the point at which we left the glacier, so we went only in light clothes and light footwear. We hugged the edge of the glacier, hopping along the piles of unstable boulders, thrust to one side by the movement of the glacier. We risked breaking an ankle or worse if a boulder should roll over, but by skirting the edge we were keeping safely away from the fall line of the seracs, the walls of ice tilting forward from the Lho La, the debris from which lay scattered across the glacier.

I was a little breathless, unaccustomed as yet to the altitude of 18,000 feet. I did not want to show my breathlessness to the twins, who are always fit as a result of their constant training sessions all the year round. Implicitly I was weighing up my partners, and felt that I was being evaluated too in terms of performance and ability. There was an unspoken bravado and tongue-in-cheek banter which seemed to acknowledge the folly of our chosen pursuit. I revelled in the company of these two brothers, feeling in no way excluded from the rapport which they had with each other.

The sun warmed the rock and, unhampered by rucksacks or heavy, warm clothing, we found ourselves scampering further and further up the gradually steepening hillside.

We had heard that this approach to the Lho La was threatened, if not by ice avalanches, then by rock avalanches. Doug Scott and Georges Bettembourg had made a foray up these slopes in 1979 and came back with awestricken tales of the lethal rockfall that showered down out of the walls above. There was indeed much evidence of newly fallen rock and no trace at all that anyone had been here before, causing us to doubt if we were heading in the right direction.

There were several buttresses of rock separated by wide gullies full of loose stones and unstable blocks. We rushed across the gullies, fearing to, be caught in them by fresh falls of rock, seeking the safety of the buttresses which stood out from the slope clear of the danger. Ade climbed up the side of one buttress thinking he had seen the obvious way up; Al and I tried another way. Once through an area of broken blocks and round a corner, we found we were on a logical progression of ledges, steps and ribs. Ade, having reached an impasse, stayed below, sheltering under a bulge of rock lest we dislodge any stones whilst climbing above him. Underfoot there was much loose rock and we realized that for safety any of us coming up here would have to stay close together. Like this, any rock dislodged could be either stopped or avoided more easily. If we were separated by long distances, anything dislodged would have a chance to gain lethal momentum and possibly strike the unwary without warning.

There was still no indication that the line we were taking would lead to the plateau of the Lho La. We were gaining height steadily, Base Camp was a tiny cluster of tents in the distance from which the echo of a voice sometimes reached us, and the hidden valley of the Western Cwm was gradually revealing itself. We were getting close to the huge walls of ice which guard access to the plateau, but in safety, to one side, we were able to look on with respect at the tortured ice formations frozen in the act of toppling over. This wall of ice, hundreds of feet high, was the end of a great bed of ice sitting on top of the rock of Everest's West Ridge. The rock is at a gentle gradient and the layer of ice is in gradual movement, slowly and inexorably sliding to the precipice beside which we were climbing. As it reaches the edge, great chunks, weighing thousands of tons, break off and crash down, scouring the gully below, and rising in a billowing cloud of ice debris which obliterates all in its path. Such avalanches are one of the nightmares of Himalayan climbing. I felt a reverential awe in gazing upon the birthplace of such colossal forces.

Al and I chased each other up the buttress; which after a jumble of loose shale, broken blocks and razor-sharp flakes had changed as we got higher to firm granite which was a pleasure to climb.

'It's like following a goat,' Al shouted up to me as I disappeared from his sight and. found we could continue even further. I did not feel as fit as a goat but could move rapidly for short lengths of time before becoming breathless. I knew that if we did too much we would exhaust ourselves and probably spend the next day recovering from headaches. It was so exciting, however, this journey of discovery, that it was impossible to resist going just that little bit further.

A steep, difficult-looking corner blocked the way, but above it the angle of the rock eased back. Al gingerly edged his way up, spreading his legs wide and balancing his toes on small rugosities in the rock. In Britain it would have been the sort of climbing we could do without thinking; here on Everest we could not help but be influenced by the situation, climbing unroped at 19,000 feet, with the debris of danger lying all around. This instilled more caution than the difficulties justified. Al found some good handholds, pulled himself onto easier ground and I followed.

A ramp led upwards to a level shoulder on the crest of the buttress and a couple of rusty tin cans. It was an encouragement that we were going the right way. A nasty looking gully of loose rock and snow separated us from some grey slabs and at the top of the wall above us we could see a line of weakness, a groove or corner, which seemed to end after about 300 feet on the Lho La plateau. It was far enough for the day. A slight breeze cooled away the warmth of the sun; without lingering further we turned to descend.

On the way down we built cairns from small rocks to mark the way for the next time we came up. Down below Ade was waiting, chilled to the bone in his light clothing. Al and I been warm enough, moving all the time. Ade had been crouched in the shadow of the bulge of rock for an hour, as we, heedless of time, had gone much further than intended. United once more, we stumbled and slid down the unstable boulders to the glacier.

From above we had noted the way back to camp across the ice. This would mean crossing the avalanche debris from the ice walls of the Lho La, but we judged that we ran a greater risk of serious injury by staying on the boulder field. Many of the boulders were precariously balanced and big enough to crush a foot or break a leg if dislodged. It took ten minutes to rush across the hard packed avalanche cone to where we guessed ourselves to be out of danger, all the while spying crevasses into which to jump and shelter should an avalanche come sweeping along.

We brought the good news of our progress back to a camp busy with activity. Brian, sleeves rolled up, pad in hand, was surrounded by boxes from which were spilling out ropes, stoves, tents and umpteen other items of equipment which he was ticking off against a list and trying to organize into readily identifiable heaps. John, dressed in strange green padded pyjamas, strutted about with a continually worried air from one pile of food to another. He broke away periodically to try to explain, with an expression of resigned patience, to Wan Chup, our cook, what each sort of food was for and how to cook it.

There seemed to be many things missing or mislaid, and the thrill I had felt at our day of discovery disappeared as we became caught up in the mundane tasks of Base Camp organization. After searching repeatedly through kitbags and boxes many things were unaccounted for. We questioned ourselves first, our own disorganization, but too many vital pieces of clothing and equipment, jacket, trousers, ice axe, were missing from different loads for it to be a coincidence. Inevitably suspicions arose about the honesty of our Sherpa staff.

In order to be free to concentrate on the climbing, and also to look after Ram Singh, our Liaison Officer, we were hiring a cook, Wan Chup, who, according to the Nepalese laws of stratification, had to have a cook boy, Mingma. We also employed another Mingma, who was to be our mail runner. To look after this group and to organize porters or yaks and any transactions with the local community we had to have a Sirdar, or head Sherpa. This was the role of Dawa, whom we had left to bring up the rear with the remaining loads.

We were completely in the hands of our Base Camp staff, as we could not keep a check on all our equipment all of the time. Fortunately Nepalese generally and the Sherpas in particular have a high reputation for honesty. On Kangchenjunga to we had handed over the money to Ang Phurba, our Sirdar; and he had hired and fired the porters as necessary; presenting us with a detailed, if crudely written, set of accounts from time to time. We therefore struggled against admitting to ourselves the possibility that this time our Base Camp staff might be dishonest.

Dawa, who was reputed to be a very capable and experienced Sherpa, arrived with the remaining loads. He resembled, with his tanned complexion, reflective sunglasses, gleaming smile and elegant clothes, a continental ski-instructor rather than a rugged man of the hills. His English was perfect. None of the missing equipment was to be found in the loads he had brought. On the contrary, more that should have been in those loads was missing.

Alan had already had a confrontation with Dawa at the very beginning when he had obviously postponed the start of the walk in for a day on the pretext of there being a hold-up with the porters. Alan had discovered that the real reason was that Dawa had wanted to spend an extra day in the company of an American girl whom he had met whilst leading a trek.

It was odious for us, amidst the raw beauty of the mountains, to have to deal with corruption which we had thought to have left behind. The Sirdar is responsible for the safe transport of the loads of his expedition. There is quite a degree of latitude in this, especially at the end of an expedition when much of the equipment is sold off cheaply or abandoned, but too much of our equipment was missing to let the matter drop.

Dawa refused to accept responsibility for any losses and insisted that everything had arrived. There was an atmosphere of discontent at Base Camp. Much energy seemed to be used up in arguments with the most sullen and uncooperative group of Sherpas I had known. The food we were eating had deteriorated from the wonderful dishes the cook was known to be capable of. There were plenty of tins of food we had brought out from Britain, but these never appeared, and our meals were a tedious affair of rice and dahl (spiced lentils). John was furious when he walked into the kitchen tent to find Dawa consuming a full tin of ham himself His explanation was that he was testing it to see whether it was suitable for himself and the rest of the Base Camp staff. At our insistence on having more than rice and dahl ourselves, the tinned food subsequently appeared on the table – the tin having been heated to thaw out the contents and placed unopened on the table with a tin opener. The cook explained this by saying that he did not know how to handle tinned foods.

It transpired that it was this same Dawa who had sown the seeds of doubt about whether Messner and Habeler had really climbed Everest without oxygen in 1978 and had gone on subsequently to accuse Messner of having stolen treasures from Nepalese monasteries some years previously. We were all uneasy about the situation; Alan felt very much the responsibility of making a decision on this. It was not a step he wanted to take lightly. If he were to dismiss Dawa it would be a serious blow to his career as a Sherpa and so far we had heard nothing but good reports on his capabilities.

Alan decided to let things stand for the moment but Base Camp was not a place I felt comfortable in with all this discord.

Undoubtedly we had been disappointed to learn that a Japanese expedition was to attempt to climb the mountain at the same time as us. Their objective was to be on the opposite side of the mountain, climbing by the South Col route, the way by which the, mountain has been climbed many times before. We knew little about their expedition until we reached Base Camp, having heard that it was an attempt at a solo ascent by Naomi Uemura. At thirty-nine, Uemura is the most famous of Japanese mountaineers and amongst other things had completed a solo crossing of the North Pole. At first it had hardly impinged on us that anyone else would be on the mountain. We imagined that Uemura's solo ascent would involve him and possibly a couple of Sherpas as Base Camp staff. Everest seemed big enough to accommodate him as well as us. It was a complete surprise on arrival, therefore, to find that there were dozens of Japanese climbers, journalists and television people occupied with this much vaunted 'solo' ascent. They also had an even larger number of Sherpas equipped to work on the mountain.

We would rather have had the mountain to ourselves but as it was we would only come into contact with the Japanese at Base Camp Their route would take them off at right angles to the direction we were going. They would have to climb up the tumbling chaos of the Khumbu icefall into the snowy valley of the Western Cwm. There they had to traverse beneath the South-West Face of the mountain to reach the opposite side to where we would be climbing. From our precarious vantage points on the way up to the Lho La, we could sometimes see the minute dots of the Japanese or their Sherpas picking their way through the maze of crevasses and toppling blocks in the icefall, as they went round to the south side of the mountain. Paradoxically, though their route is the easiest way up, gaining it entails crossing the most dangerous and area of the mountain.

The Japanese were neighbours, camped only a few hundred yards away, Alan went over to pay a courtesy call. He came back with an invitation for all of us to go across in the evening for a meal. It promised to be a welcome change from rice and dahl.

The Japanese tents were in a slight hollow, not completely visible from our camping place. From above a swelling in the surface of the glacier could be seen the many pinnacles of their orange tents. It looked to be an enormous camp. Towards evening, well insulated for a short journey, we trooped across in the direction of their lights.

On closer acquaintance the many pinnacles appeared to be clustered closely together; my perception could not resolve what, I was seeing. A large tent flap opened, spilling electric light out onto the ice, and we stumbled inside after each other, blinded by the unexpected brightness. We were inside a huge marquee. The pinnacles were not closely grouped tents after all, but one enormous tent with many points, the like of which I had never seen before. Outside an electric generator throbbed away and a string of glowing bulbs ran the whole length of this, grandiose construction. The chimney of a wood-burning stove disappeared upwards to be lost in the voluminous folds of the tent's inner lining, and a long, low narrow table ran the length of the room with armchairs made from bamboo cane on either side of it.

Sometimes I have the sensation that I am no longer contributing to events, but am being controlled by them as they happen. I couldn't grasp what was happening – Everest, winter, cold and discomfort and suddenly we were in a cocoon of luxury, surrounded by smiling faces, flashing, whirring cameras and microphones, warm and comfortable. Some small plastic bottles were produced from a box and Naomi Uemura, grinning broadly, said: 'This is Saki. We bring to celebrate our summit climb. But now we celebrate you coming.'

We all drank and sat and grinned. More details of this unbelievable tent registered in my mind. I did not like to stare – I felt as if I was in someone's private rooms. Along each wall was a row of curtained alcoves perhaps six feet long by four feet wide. These were the sleeping places for the Japanese members, with a thin partition of nylon as a concession to privacy. At the furthest end of the tent was a bank of electrical consoles. 'Is that a hi-fi system?' one of our team asked hopefully. 'No, it is a facsimile machine for weather reports from Delhi.'

The cost of transporting all of this equipment must have been enormous. Only the name of Uemura had made it possible as the expedition was backed by a Japanese TV company and newspaper.

I was interested to meet Uemura. The chubby-faced, boyish looks gave no suggestion of the man's acknowledged hardiness, nor of the determination which had driven him during the many months of his solo Arctic crossing.

'How is Don Whillan? Is he still climbing?' Uemura had spent much time with Don on Everest's South-West Face in 1971.

He seemed at ease, with a youthful enjoyment of drinking and joking. It was not the hardship he must have put up with in the Arctic crossing but the deadly boredom of months of solitude which I found amazing.

'Are you married? What does your wife think of you spending so much time away?'

'My wife is very happy for me.'

The Japanese were interested in our ages. Uemura felt, at thirty-nine, that he was coming to the end of his active years.

His expedition also had a scientific project, with three scientists taking bore samples from the glacier and sending them back to Kathmandu. Two doctors, a journalist and a film crew completed the team. Uemura had spent some weeks in the region during the winter of 1979/80 and had realized the importance of having a comfortable Base Camp. For this reason he had returned to Japan where he had two purpose-built tents made to withstand the wind and cold.

Further down the table other members of our team were having different conversations. There were a number of other Japanese climbers on the expedition, one of whom said: 'I have contract to go to 200 metres from summit. After that only Mr Uemura goes alone.'

Someone was talking to the Sirdar of the Japanese Sherpas: 'The British expedition will reach top of mountain before Japanese, because Japanese use Sherpas who want money and so make expedition last longer.'

We had stumbled into the tent blinded by the light, now we stumbled out, drunk from the unaccustomed quantities of alcohol, thanking our hosts profusely. Course after course of strange delicacies had appeared before us, most of which I found myself picking at and discreetly leaving to one side. I noticed most of our team doing the same. Our digestive systems had still scarcely adjusted to the altitude and the food we were more familiar with; to have forced down exotic morsels, with to us a bizarre taste, would have invited disaster. I hoped that we had not caused mortal offence in terms of the Japanese code of conduct, but there was no way to tell from their excessive demonstrations of politeness and goodwill.

Back at our own camp we separated each to his own tent.

The Japanese set-up was certainly a contrast. As I slid, fully dressed, into my sleeping bag, the thermometer read: -11 degrees Celsius!

On Tuesday 9 December John Porter joined the Burgess twins and myself in going back up towards the Lho La. There were still many jobs to do round Base Camp and four was quite enough at one time to be working on the route. It also gave those who had been struck down with dysentery a chance to regain their strength.

More familiar this time with the way, we lost no time in reaching the high point of the previous day. Al, moving powerfully on ahead, skirted below a wall of rock and traversed back above it. John and I were below as he crossed a slope of loose stones, sending showers of them down onto us. I was out of line of fire, but John was caught in the open, cursing loudly as the stones bounced off his helmet. Al stopped moving as we shouted abuse at him and stayed motionless and looking apologetically sheepish until we had caught him up. We did not let ourselves get separated again.

We had brought a rucksack each full of rope to fix in place on the more difficult ground. We would have to go up and down many times before we were finished with the mountain, so to save time and ensure safety we had brought rope to leave as a handline where it was necessary, once we had climbed a section. On the biggest mountains it is hardly possible to climb continuously upwards day after day. A period of acclimatization is essential. We did not have a fully predetermined plan about how to climb the mountain, but we were finding that the best method was to fix rope on the difficult ground. Sometimes we only climbed a few hundred feet a day, but with rope once fixed in place, ascent was much more rapid. To have placed a camp after only a few hundred feet would have been futile and would have necessitated carrying enormous weights of tentage, food and equipment. By linking together the efforts of each day to place a camp only after a major section was completed, we gave ourselves a chance of acclimatizing in the process and made a more economical use of our resources.

An area of grey, granite slabs stretched up out of the evil looking gully at which we had stopped the day before. I stayed back filming the other three as they scurried across the broken, rocky bed of the gully to a promontory on the far side. Being in the bottom of the gully held the sensation of being in the bottom of a rubbish chute, a focal point for anything thrown from above. The gully was an alien place. We felt much more at ease on the smooth, grey slabs above.

These were not difficult, but it would save time, when carrying a heavy load, to have a rope in place, and if it should snow heavily there were other places where we might need fixed ropes.

It had been another clear, fine day when we had left. Rapidly it had changed; the ambient air temperature was always well below freezing point, and it was only the heat of the sun which gave the impression that a day was warm. Once the sun was masked by cloud, or a wind started, the bitterness of winter made itself felt. By the time we had reached the grey slabs we were cold. For once the Burgess twins, usually so careful, were caught unawares, and as soon as they had used up the rope out of their sacks they rushed off down to avoid the danger of exposure.

John and I, better clothed, were able to continue. John felt guiltily responsible for the weather. The Sherpas had caught him burning some rubbish at Base Camp that morning and had given him a ticking off: They had said it was bad to burn rubbish as it brought bad weather. John viewed his handiwork with a resigned air. None of us is really superstitious but on a mountain, when in a state of nervous tension, one can be susceptible to anything that is said or held with conviction. On Kangchenjunga we had not walked the last ten feet to the summit as the people of Sikkim believe this would desecrate the home place of the gods they believe live there and cause them to send floods and earthquakes in revenge. We did not see any gods and did not hold these beliefs, but an ominous storm was approaching the mountain and a huge black bird hung over the summit watching us. No word had passed, but none of us thought to trespass further.

John has a slight, stooping build, belying a tough resilience. As I got to know him I realized that his quietness was reflective. He was what I would consider to be an intellectual, nurturing his knowledge and reproducing it at the most apt moments. He has an apologetic manner which conceals the strengths which motivate him, and which earned him the respect of the Poles with whom he had taken to climbing after a visit to Poland as part of an official exchange group of mountaineers.

As he descended a precarious ramp into yet another horrifying gully I was glad that he seemed unperturbed at the prospect before us. This gully was steeper, encircled at the top by a basin of convoluted ice. How steep it was, was hard to judge, and secretly, with the cowardliness of innermost thoughts, I hoped that John would have enough rope to get the measure of the difficulties before I took over.

He climbed along the edge of the gully, up onto the ice as far as he could go. I joined him and he led off again, this time forced into the bed of the gully, a runnel with dirty smears on the ice where rocks had struck on their way down. More loose blocks were balanced one on top of another and John eased his way past them, his legs spread wide across the narrowed funnel of rock which reared up out of the top rim of the ice. He went out of sight, the rope still Moving slowly upwards, then came the sound of the hammering of pitons into rock and a shout for me to come.

It was my turn to go first, I had to cross the gully and climb the opposite wall of ice to an overhanging rock groove which appeared to end on the crest of the ridge and at the Lho La. The ice still looked steep, even from close to, and I felt nervous.

A thirty-foot-high step of rock blocked the way to the ice; it required some delicate moves, awkward in the huge, clumsy boots I was wearing. I felt the surge of nervous excitement as I moved tentatively upwards on small footholds to where I could place a piton and achieve some security. The ice was steep but it was pockmarked with weather-worn holes into which I could step, and a few projecting rocks frozen into place provided the infrequent handhold. As usual the encounter was not as frightening as the anticipation. I reached the bottom of the rock wall running into the overhanging groove and secured the rope.

Above I could see signs of the Yugoslav expedition – the remnants of a wire ladder and frayed ropes. The 300-foot groove above clearly presented considerable difficulties. It was late in the afternoon, we had used all our rope and I turned to descend.

The following day Paul, Brian and Pete, carrying heavy loads of rope, went up to make a cache of equipment ready for the major assault on the groove and the anticipated breakthrough onto the Lho La. They were now recovered from the illness, having only coughs and sore throats which the cold, dry air continued to irritate. Alan had been hit worst by the dysentery and was fighting hard to shake off the sickness which was sapping his strength. He busied himself at Base Camp with calculations of the expedition's finances, food and fuel consumption and general estimations of our progress. The sickness was going right through the camp; Ade was next taken ill.

Five of us went up next; Al and John fastened themselves into the overhanging groove preparing for a long siege. Brian and Pete laboured up with more loads, signalling their movements with periodic bursts of noisy coughing. I lodged myself onto a ledge on the opposite side of the gully with a movie camera and watched Al's distant, matchstick moves up the yellow rock.

The remains of the wire ladder hung temptingly down the groove, but the wire was frayed and the rungs bent and twisted either from rockfall or winds. I could see Al testing it and hesitatingly groping his way upwards on the rock with grunts and pauses for breath, preferring to climb the rock which he could rely on than trust to an abandoned hawser. His muffled exchanges with John belaying him carried across the gully; it was clear that he was having a struggle.

Some rock broke away from under of his foot and ricocheted across the gully to just below where I was sitting. John looked over to me. Neither of us said anything; there was nothing to say.

The groove and the wall up which Al was finding the way, was exceptionally difficult climbing for the altitude. It looked as if it might be technically the most interesting climbing on the route. We would not be able to cope with anything as difficult as this higher up the mountain, as the ever more rarefied air would not sustain the strenuous efforts required. I was partly envious and partly relieved that someone else was leading this section. I would have liked the satisfaction of solving this particularly difficult problem first, but there were other essential roles to play; I was filming the ascent for ITN; Brian and Pete were carrying loads in support, possibly the most tedious and unrecognized contribution to any expedition. Given that with honour I could sit back, I did feel a guilty self-indulgence at watching someone else struggling to force a way up the rock and fix rope in place for everyone else to follow.

The gully was deep and caught the heat of the sun. The wind did not penetrate but could be heard whistling over the top of the ridge, a few hundred feet above. The heat of the sun loosened some rocks; with increasing frequency stones began to fall past my eyrie. Had the stones been falling when I had arrived there I would not have stayed but I had been there half an hour before the first fell and had come to feel at home. It was slow progress up the groove; I did not want to miss filming the last moments as Al moved up onto the ridge, and I sat for three hours, pressing myself hard against the rock behind me to avoid the stones which by the end were falling every ten minutes. Once Al knocked down a massive block which shattered on impact and sprayed all around me. John looked helplessly on.

Al reached a ledge at half height and John climbed up the rope to join him, using jumar clamps which slide up the rope and locked, taking most of the difficulty out of the ascent: The second half of the wall went more quickly and a jubilant Al shouted down that he had reached a platform, but not the Lho La.

I was as relieved as he was; I could quit the perch in the firing range and ferry my load up to the top of the ropes Al had fixed in place. It was indeed an impressive performance by Al, as I realized on reaching the groove. The first bit was overhanging and, even with the ropes, very strenuous. It took me an hour to climb the wall and join John and Al. Pete and Brian appeared in the gully below and I warned them to stay clear on account of the falling stones.

Enough had been achieved for the day. Short of energy and time we returned to Base Camp: Psychologically it was very good to have overcome such a major obstacle, though further difficult ground barred the way to the plateau. If the whole route continued as hard and slow as this section it boded ill for our chances.

We sat in our dining tent discussing tactics and experiences. The tent was shabby and cold by comparison with the Japanese pavilion. We had one small paraffin stove on the table to give a semblance of heat, but it was necessary to wear padded clothing even inside. Huddled together round the yellow light mountain. The film team had been strangely inactive for a while; I began to wonder if they were being affected by the altitude and slipping into a routine which made it seem as if there was not enough time to do everything, but proved a tendency to put off doing anything until another occasion. Many expedition films fail to succeed entirely on account of this – just surviving on a daily basis at Base Camp can be quite exhausting enough. Allen Jewhurst, director of the film, however, had gone up to the start of the fixed ropes in the company of the lead party, to weigh up camera positions. Unfamiliar with the route, he had sat and waited till Paul, who was making a short carry with a load to the start of the fixed ropes, arrived and descended with him.

It was dusk when John, looking worn and weary, burst into the dining tent where the rest of us were settling into our places for the evening. A growing anxiety at the late return of everyone from the hill was immediately relieved. John sank down onto a box for a seat and questions about the day's climbing started. John has a. way of not answering questions immediately nor in the way expected.

'The others aren't going to get here before dark, I don't think they've got torches and they are short of a pair of crampons.'

Everyone looked at him; they were not the words expected in answer to the questions. My mind ran over a checklist of essentials and their whereabouts – ice axe, crampons, torch, spare torch, mitts, boots Brian next to me seemed to be doing the same. John took the silence for reluctance to stir out into the cold night: 'Look, those guys have been working hard all day and are struggling down in the dark. Are you going to sit here on your arses? They need torches to get across the glacier. I'd go back but I'm knackered.'

It was a startling outburst. John, fully dressed for the cold outside, still with his crampons on, did not realize that anyone going out into the night would have to get ready. It might take ten minutes, it might take two hours to locate and return with the other three, but to venture out unprepared invited disaster. Bare hands would be numb in minutes.

Brian and I scratched around in the dark inside and outside our tents, trying to remember where things were, and, prepared as best we could, hurried urgently over uneven ground towards the slopes up the Lho La. The night was still but there was no sound carried on the air; tragedy in the mountains can occur from the most innocuous situation, and flutterings of unease tightened my stomach. Where the ice was no longer roughened by rubble we stopped and strapped crampons to our boots to allow, us, to walk more easily on the undulating, glistening surface. We followed the pools of light cast by our torches along the marks on the ice made by the earlier passage of our feet and then, unheralded, the chattering voices of swaying figures rose up from out of a hollow to meet us. There was laughter and ribald curses from the trio making me feel foolish for the anxiety I had felt for them.

They were tired and indeed had no torch; Alan and Al were sharing a pair of crampons – one boot each securely bound with a row of metal spikes to give purchase on the ice, the other, rubber-soled, slipping and unbalancing their gait, making a mockery of any pretensions to be experienced mountaineers.

There was a warm comradeship in our meeting.

'Thanks for coming to meet us, lads,' said Ade, 'it's really been hard work getting across in the dark.'

We returned together to camp, seeing the dining tent now as a cosy haven by comparison with the outside world.

I awoke from a disturbing dream in which I was hanging by the neck and a vision of failure on the route. There were no grounds for these unsettling dreams except that I had gone to sleep with a familiar feeling of apprehension before embarking on the next stage of the climb, the next step into the unknown.

Movement and a sense of fitness banished such chimeras in the bright light of day. I reached the top of the fixed ropes by 1.30 p.m.; weighed down by a sack which held, in addition to the essentials for a stay of two or three nights, 40 pounds of food and gear. Paul and Brian, similarly laden; were also toiling up the ropes to stay.

We planned to start digging a snow cave and, if this was not big enough to sleep in by evening, to erect a tent for the night. We had little hope of a tent lasting very long in the winds of the Lho La, but hoped to dispense with it after one night. There was nowhere in sight that seemed suitable to start digging a cave. Hard, icy snow swept upwards at too precarious an angle for siting a cave. Rationalizing the situation, I knew that we would not do any digging at all this day, there was still some gear to be picked up from the cache at the top of the corner and there was not even a place where we could put up a tent.

Dumping my sack, I scrambled upwards on easier ground, kicking the edge of my boot into the snow and holding onto the rock against which it abutted. It was a foolish but delightful romp, liberated from the weight of my sack and the constriction of being fastened into a rope. I would not be allowed even one slip, not one error of judgement, but I had the strength and confidence of fitness, reaching up and testing each handhold before pulling up on it; kicking a boot into the snow and trying my weight on that foot before committing myself to it completely. The enthusiasm was rewarded; a broad ledge, ten feet wide, opened up to my left. It was littered with rocks, easily wide enough for a tent and the rocks could be made into a wall as a wind-break. Reassured at this alternative to a frantic attempt at excavating a snow cave as a shelter for the night, I turned to descend and propose the change of plan to Paul and Brian.

I had not looked down as I climbed upwards above the ropes. As I turned now and saw the ice runnel up which I had come, ending abruptly at the edge of the precipice of the amphitheatre, I felt sick and nervous at the insecurity of my position. I descended the 200 feet back to the ropes with my stomach knotted in apprehension, clutching more tightly than was warranted to every hold, inescapably aware of the folly of my situation.

Paul had reached the end of the ropes when I arrived back. He agreed that it would be most sensible to pitch a tent immediately than risk having no-shelter ready by nightfall.

'Did you pick the tent up? I couldn't find it.'

'No, I looked in one of the sacks half way up the corner, it wasn't in there.'

'Damn, I wonder if Brian's got it.'

'What's it like up to the ledge?'

'OK, but be careful. You'll be safer with crampons on.'

I slid down the ropes strung along the rim of the amphitheatre and regained the top of the corner with a pleasurable ease which made ridiculous the effort needed to climb upwards on the same ground. I could hear Brian long before I could see him, as his hacking coughs echoed up the corner.

There was no tent with the gear at the top of the corner and Brian didn't have it either. I slid down the ropes of the corner, imagining an ignominious retreat if there was no tent to be found and dreading the long haul back up the ropes if there was.

The tent was concealed in a sack which-Paul had not examined; I shouldered the sack and started back up.

The preliminary plan of digging a snow cave for the night had been absurdly ambitious; we had barely time to erect the tent, build a protective wall of rocks and gather snow to melt for the evening meal before sunset and the rapid night took over.

Brian was weary from the journey up. He sank into the dark interior of the tent, thrusting out a grateful hand for mugs of liquid and plates of food as they were prepared. Sometimes his pained face would appear in the light of the stove as he strained forward, shaken by another spasm of coughing.

Heavy-boned and big-framed, Brian gave me, as I grew to know him, the impression that he was always pushing himself hard. If it was recounting lurid stories, Brian strove to produce the most startling; if it was outrageous behaviour, Brian would outgross anyone. On the mountain I could see him driving himself on against the affliction of his crippling cough long after I would have let myself turn back. Brian was continually forcing himself along the road of excess in his search for the palace of wisdom. I imagined his throat to be raw and bleeding.

Again the night was suspiciously calm. I was numb when I crawled back from the edge of the platform from where I had been futilely attempting to make a radio call to Base Camp thousands of feet below, but only the lightest breeze rocked the tent. Our platform was awesomely poised on the very brink of a precipice, but somehow tucked away from the wind streaming across the Lho La plateau. We spent a restless night, the three of us pressed close together, suffocated with the tent door closed and chilled with it open. Next day I had a headache and the three of us were slow to make a start.

To find a more level area of snow in which we could dig a cave without risk of slipping down a steep slope as soon as one stepped outside, we headed for the plateau of the Lho La itself. A basin of firm snow, split by a number of crevasses, gave way to easier angled slopes that descended to level ground. I was ready to go and Paul suggested I lead off, fixing rope onto aluminium stakes driven into the snow until I was no longer above the gulf of the amphitheatre. There was no advantage to the climbing in having a rope there, but we would have to cross and recross this slope many times, and it would be so much safer with a hand rail in place. Without a fixed rope, a gust of wind could overbalance someone and throw him down the slope into the amphitheatre.

I was nervous of starting off, the slope of snow looked steep, but it was an optical illusion, the yawning abyss a hundred feet below influencing my view of the situation. When I was clear of the abyss, I drove a final stake into the snow and shouted to Paul and Brian to follow.

The snow slope I was on cased down for three hundred feet into a level plateau; this in turn swept northwards and down, losing itself in a jagged maze of ice pinnacles; remote, mysterious Tibet lay brown in the distance. Across the plateau rose the icy escarpment of the West Ridge, 3,500 feet of snow, rock and ice to the rounded dome of the shoulder. Lurking elusively, a thrilling sight behind the Western Shoulder, was the summit – so far away. A banner of cloud streamed off it, the symbol of winter, barren and windy. That was our objective but, as usual, I found myself shelving any thought of what was to come and concentrated on the task of the moment.

Brian had spent the summer in the Karakoram at the other end of the Himalayas taking part in the ski descent of Baltoro Kangri. He was enthusiastic about a snow cave they had dug there which, according to the description, sounded like a palace. Paul and. I, professing less experience in such matters, looked to Brian for suggestions as to the best place, and method of construction.

There was a science to it; an optimum angle of slope; a method of achieving the correct lengths of entry into the slope before starting to form a chamber. It was hard work, there was no science about that. We were at 20,000 feet and the maximum spell of digging that any of us could do was ten to fifteen minutes. We took it in turns.

John and Ade arrived in the course of the day while Brian and Paul were digging and I was having a rest. 'You're foreman are you?' Ade joked when he came, watching shovels full of snow being ejected from the hole.

They brought news of Pete injecting the cook boy with an anti-nausea drug; the sickness seemed to be circulating round the camp. Alan was ill again and Al had gone down with the same thing. Usually on an expedition all germs seem to disappear. It is so cold that they are killed off or rendered inactive.

This time, however, in spite of the cold, we seemed to be afflicted by a particularly virulent strain, and once the sickness took hold, recovery was very much harder.

John and Ade did not stay long. They dumped their loads and hurried down. By 4 p.m. we had dug out a cave, big enough for one person. The snow was hard, ideal for climbing, taking only the front points of the crampons to give a secure foothold, but tiresome for digging. The early stages were the worst as the entrance had to be a narrow tunnel to keep out as much wind as possible, which meant that only one of us could work, sometimes on knees, sometimes lying flat, working away under showers of ice splinters. It did not look much for a day's work but there was room now for two people kneeling upright to dig all the time, and next day we expected progress to be much quicker with a habitable snow cave by the time we finished.

Somehow I was manoeuvred into being cook again, a laborious task with much of the time being taken up just melting snow to get the liquid to make a meal or a drink. From start to finish, in order to obtain the necessary bodily intake of fluid, cooking a meal can take three or more hours. I kept dozing off whilst waiting for the snow to melt and the water to boil. The boiling point of water at high altitude is much lower than at sea level. Due to the decreased air pressure, the water, vaporizes at a lower temperature, but the heat is not there to cook the food. Most things take three times as long to cook as at sea level.

'Does one of you two want to have a go?'

'You seem better acclimatized than us – we need the rest!'

I realized how Dick Renshaw must have felt on K2 when Pete and I had languished in our sleeping bags whilst he, uninfluenced by any mood of lethargy, used to be up first thing preparing breakfast to get us moving. There is some mechanism of passive resistance on expeditions which conspires to instil a reluctance to make more effort than absolutely necessary, so that making a cup of tea can come to seem like a monstrous task. Yet more than on any other expedition the dehydration effect of altitude and cold was making it essential to drink more than the accepted minimum of eight pints a day and to force oneself to eat whether one felt like it or not. Without the liquid, altitude sickness and headaches occur much more readily, and without the food we would be weak and much more susceptible to the cold.

After another fitful night we worked on the snow cave until the middle of the afternoon. We were weary now and my fatigued muscles seemed to be contributing little to the enlargement of the cave. Al arrived and I followed him down to Base Camp, having dismantled the tent lest it should be blown away by the wind. Paul and Brian followed later. There was the warm ache of tiredness in my legs as I crossed the glacier back to camp and the thicker air of Base Camp made me drowsy. Alan, worn out by his debilitating sickness, looked jaded and depressed.

We now had a base for action on the West Ridge itself. The ascent up to the Lho La had been technically much more difficult than we had expected, and more difficult than anything else we hoped to find higher up. It felt to me like a preparation, an essential and unavoidable part of the climb, but nonetheless only a preparation, and that it was from the Lho La that I would begin to feel that real progress was being made. For the three of us who had been up there it was time for a rest but I envied the discoveries that those who were going up next would make as they explored new ground.

6 Progress and Punishment

The mail runner arrived while we were on the mountain. With the welcome letters was the surprise of a newspaper, *The Observer*, three weeks late but a prized arrival all the same, complete with colour supplement. We were sending back news reports to *The Observer* and they had agreed to mail to us a copy each week during the expedition. I spent a whole day leisurely soaking up every bit of world news, cinema critiques, book reviews and even business news. It mattered little that it was all three weeks out of date.

Our shy little Liaison Officer, glued to his radio for much of the day, sometimes volunteered a snippet of news, or the Japanese passed on something they had picked up on their radio. It was thus we came to learn of, and be shocked unaccountably by John Lennon's death. There was a strange sense of *déjà vu* in this two-stage arrival of news. One associates newspapers with almost the same instantaneous transmission of news as the radio or television. For us the time-lag between the two was so great that the news from the radio had passed into the subconscious long before the, paper arrived, so that I read *The Observer* with an uncanny and mistaken sensation of prescience.

There was no organized manner in which we went up on the mountain. In keeping with the democratic ideals of the expedition it was held that everyone was capable enough and experienced enough to make decisions themselves on the mountain; everyone was mature enough to work to his maximum and consequently there was no need for any, direction of effort. Thus there was no order in which anyone went up to carry loads or occupy the snow cave or push the route further. Not everyone was in agreement over this. The Burgess twins were vociferous in their condemnation of what they called 'random attack'; John believed that everyone should do a certain number of trips just carrying loads up to the Lho La before moving up. Alan was adamant that everyone was working to his limit and that no more could be expected: 'There may be an uneven distribution of what is being done at the moment, but by the end of the trip it will all have balanced out.' Nevertheless, there was feeling in some quarters that more organization and coordination would not be a bad thing.

The Burgess twins, John and Pete moved up to occupy and enlarge the snow cave. Two of them stayed in the tent, for a night until a second adjoining cave was dug, making ample space for all eight of us. They made the mistake of leaving the tent up on a windy night and on the next day, going to ferry some gear across from it to the caves, found it collapsed. The 'unbreakable' fibreglass poles had been eroded away by the action of the wind shaking the tent incessantly throughout a night and rubbing the poles against a rock used to hold the tent down. Inside the snow cave only the sound of the wind penetrated as a distant drone and it was possible to forget its power and persistence.

At Base Camp, intermittently resting and carrying loads up to the Lho La, I was hard put to decide on the best way of utilizing a rest day. The hours of sun were so short and life outside those, hours was a misery. The meal times were the focal points of the day, starting with the rattling of pans and kettles in the early morning, signifying the preparation of 'bed tea', the most welcome tradition established by the great pioneers of Himalayan mountaineering. Before the day can start, the ritual of tea being brought round and thrust with a grinning 'Morning, sahib, tea' into the tent has to take place. One feels its absence with an irritation similar to that when the milkman has somehow failed to deliver and a cheerless breakfast with black coffee and no cereal starts the day. It is as if it is a God-given right and impossible to stir from the sleeping bag without it. But once the tea arrives and the whole, hot pint swallowed, it is not many minutes before there is a series of scufflings and pulling of cords and zips as everyone is forced to rush outside to relieve a full bladder. The worst situation occurs when the bio-rhythms are not properly-regulated or a pre-dawn sortie into a chill world is brought on by the Pavlovian rattle of kettles and cups from the cook tent.

The dining tent was the centre of the camp, the place where we socialized, discussed, bragged, argued and ate. I felt isolated in my own tent, but unable to concentrate in the dining tent if I wanted to read and there were conversations going on.

One discussion revolved around tactics on the mountain. Alan was all in favour of using snow caves all the way. He and Brian had been part of a team that had climbed the North Face of Nuptse in 1979 and had been impressed with the use of snow caves there. I believed that he was underestimating the difficulty involved in digging snow caves at altitude and said that we would need a cave for at least six people on the West Shoulder at about 23,000 feet and four people at 25,000 feet. I calculated this on the basis of having a rotation of people on the mountain both for digging the caves in the first place and going to the summit at the end. Unless there was accommodation for at least four people at 25,000 feet there would be a gap of several days between one pair going for the top and the next pair.

The twins descended from the Lho La and discussion turned towards the summit. Faced with the overwhelming reality of Everest in winter, fanciful ideas bandied around in England disappeared and now Al voiced his opinion: 'I think that it's going to need all our efforts to get two people to the top. There's no way we are all going to get there. Two of us getting up will be good

Having gained some confidence about moving about on the easier ground, and familiarity with the route in the lower part of the rock buttress before the ropes started, the film crew were in the habit of venturing up themselves to find vantage points for their cameras. The debate on their role had not been concluded. There was still some uneasiness amongst the climbers about leaving the film crew alone on the mountain, and it was as difficult for us to judge how hard it was for them to cope with ground we covered as a matter of routine as it is for someone who can drive to imagine the difficulties someone sees who cannot drive. Much later, Allen Jewhurst described an incident fully justifying our fears:

> A lot of thoughts go through one's mind in fifteen seconds. Our cameraman, Mike Shrimpton, was sliding down a slope with a drop of 1,500 feet below him. We had decided to reconnoitre the route up to the Lho La and find good camera positions. It was also a reasonably safe area to see how well Graham, our sound recordist, could cope with the climbing. I had climbed the route with Peter three days earlier. After three hours we found ourselves in a disconcerting situation. At 19,000 feet we had drifted off the route and were lost. We told Graham to stay put on a rib of rock on the left of a gully. Mike was to search out to the right and I to the left. After a few minutes I recognized the route to my left, over a rise. As I turned to call Mike, I saw him sliding down the gully. A loose rock had given way and he was falling towards Graham. Mike was a goner, I was sure, and what of Graham? If left alive with Mike dead, how would he react? Graham had never climbed in his life before and here he was at 19,000 feet with his friend falling to his death.
>
> Graham watched astounded. Mike stretched out his arms, clawing as he fell, his fingers caught on a lip of rock and he came to a halt against Graham. With precise calmness, Mike politely told Graham to move a foot to the right. He took over Graham's perch and fifteen minutes later we were back on route with two decisions made: not to get lost again and not to tell the climbers.

Base Camp was a world away from life on the mountain; the difference was as great as that between life in Britain and life at Base Camp. For the first 1,500 feet on the ice slopes the climbers were out of sight. I had inherited the duty of making the radio calls and my conception of those on the mountain was influenced by the tiny, crackling voices which came over the radio. Without realizing it, I associated the little voices with the minute figures last glimpsed through a telephoto lens, climbing slowly up to the Lho La, and half imagined my friends on the mountain to have become matchstick men. It was a foolish flight of fancy brought on by the enormity of our objective.

The twins and John arrived down with details of their progress above the Lho La and information on the line which Brian and Pete were intending to try through the rock barrier. They were awed by the effort required for the distance they had covered, by the relentless cold, even though the sky might be clear, and by the work which remained.

The film crew had an enormous lens mounted on one of their cameras and someone was forever peering through it to see if there was any sign of Brian and Pete. An excited shout went up when they were spotted; invisible to the naked eye they appeared as real people through the powerful lens, though it was only possible to distinguish them from each other by the colour of their clothing. I felt as if I was peeping in on a private, personal conflict. The two matchstick figures were close together. The red one, Brian, was above the other; from his questing movements I could see he was having difficulty. A telescoped view can be deceptive, making some things look easier, some harder; by all indications this was a crucial section with which they were struggling, and Brian described how it was.

> I felt cold and quite remote from mankind. Base Camp, the tiny coloured dots on the glacier far below, was a different world. Standing here, hour after hour it seemed, as Pete led across steep ice and into the rock band, I had time to reflect on our isolation and remoteness. Already the 'norm' had become Base Camp life, a 'norm' far removed from a life surrounded by the conveniences and comforts of our civilization.
>
> Pete was having problems, finding himself being forced leftwards as one icy groove after another resisted his attempts to climb it. I was impatient with Pete's slow progress, feeling the urge to have a go myself and having to refrain from making what I thought would be helpful suggestions. As time passed, I became bored with the depressing scene of cloud dropping lower and lower over Pumori and Gyachung Kang, and the view down the Rongbuk glacier to the barren hills of Tibet. A twenty-six-mile marathon could be run in less time, I reflected, than it had taken us to climb up the 1,500 feet to this point.
>
> Paradoxically, this was just the opportunity I had been waiting for. I had been ill for the first few weeks of the trip with a bronchial complaint aggravated by the dry, cold air. Plagued by an incessant cough, my role until today had been one of supporting and load-carrying for the fitter members. Illness and

constant load-carrying were not what my expedition dreams were made from. Visions of surmounting difficult ice gullies, smooth slabs of rock and steep snow slopes, dreams of leading the way for rope length after rope length, had all been shattered; shattered by sickness and drudgery. Some of the team were fulfilling their dreams. I had not been, and I was questioning my own ability to cope with such a difficult route and such harsh conditions.

This time on the mountain I had started well, reaching. Camp 1 quicker than I had ever done, and was enthusiastic at the prospect of breaking through the rock band. Now it was getting late, an earlier headache and grogginess had passed off but the wind was gaining in strength and the cloud, was thickening. Impatience at the late hour conflicted with impatience to be leading myself. I was excited to realize that when it was my turn I should break through this impasse to the easier ground above.

With Pete finally established on a poor ledge but firmly fastened to pitons driven into rock, I followed eagerly. Where Pete had had to climb carefully, axes planted in ice, crampon points grating on rock, I, safeguarded by the rope, tried to hurry and generate some warmth. My lungs almost burst; I became light-headed and dizzy through trying to force myself without sufficient oxygen. I arrived at the ledge in a tangle of ropes. My mind was as active as a garden snail, my hands without feeling from the cold – it took was a long time to untangle the ropes.

When I started up the ice gully from the ledge, the dizziness returned; I climbed more slowly. From the top of the gully, I saw the solution to the problem of surmounting the final overhangs. An undercut ledge ran left to a bottomless corner of rock. This ran up to the barrier of rock which overhung this area at the narrowest point. If I could get through the overhang here; we would be on easier ground and a major obstacle would have been conquered.

Leaving the groove I was in to gain the ledge felt extremely precarious, and the 'high' of leading was soon shattered by terror as my arms rapidly tired and the prospect of hurtling backwards down the groove loomed large. I gained the ledge with my last strength, but the strain of the previous few minutes had unnerved me so much that what I had thought a large platform now seemed barely wide enough to catch the points of my crampons. I could not rest, but clung on for dear life. 'Watch the rope, Pete,' I shouted down. 'I'll try to get a peg in.' The peg went all too easily into a crack in the rock, seeming to prise the rock away with it, but it gave me confidence and I edged left to the corner.

The corner was clogged with snow but I could rest; my terror was forgotten and I was beginning to enjoy the day. Down below it was Pete now who looked bored, fidgeting and stamping his feet impatiently. For him, I knew, time would be passing slowly. For me, time did not exist; the climbing engrossed me completely.

I cleared the snow from the corner, discovering plenty of holds, and reached the overhang quickly. After a rest, a heave upwards and a swing left landed me on the easy ground above.

There was a sense of fulfilment, a sense of achievement, but now that I was over the difficulty time did matter; night was near, wind-blown snow obscured the view down to the Lho La and the urgency of the situation made itself felt. I waited till Pete had arrived and dumped his load and we hurried off down.

Abseil followed abseil till we reached the easier slopes as darkness fell. The way back to the cave of Camp 1 was vague in the mist and dark. Several times we were blown off course by the wind and it was with relief that we chanced upon the debris of our food packages and the gentle rise up to the cave.

It was 22 December. Alan, Paul and I planned to go up the next day to take over from Brian and Pete, whom we expected to be, tired after breaking through the rock barrier. I awoke on 23 December to steady snowfall and low cloud. The radio call to Pete and Brian told us that conditions were too bad to climb at the time; if the weather cleared they, would do some more, if not they would enlarge the cave further and dig a snow-hole toilet, to make living conditions more bearable at Camp 1, before coming down to Base Camp. We decided not to go up ourselves until the weather cleared and I felt a guilty thrill that we might after all be at Base Camp to celebrate Christmas, and receive the next batch of mail that was due. If the weather did clear there was no question but that we would go up, whatever the sentimental attraction of celebrating Christmas, as fine days were too precious and irretrievable to pass up.

The snowfall did not let up all day; heavy, persistent. Flakes brought a hushed whiteness to the camp. Brian and Pete shoved their way through the drapes of the dining tent entrance towards evening, covered in snow, and still wearing crampons. Brian was gasping hard as if he had just survived an Arctic epic; Pete, controlled, strode across the tent and with measured slowness unfastened his crampons and sat down.

This was the first real encounter that any of us had had with the mountain in severe conditions and Brian's description of their descent from the snow cave gave a disconcerting impression of the forces with which we were contending.

The storm of the previous evening had worsened during the night. We guessed that no one would come up from Base Camp in such weather and Pete and I resolved to descend as quickly as possible. We did not know what it would be like to be caught in a winter storm on the mountain, and the possibility of being stranded for days seemed very real.

I left first and had difficulty standing upright against the wind as soon as I was out of the cave. The rope ran up the slope from the mouth of the cave for 200 feet to a snow stake. From there it went horizontally for another 300 feet to the first rocks from where the descent proper began. I clipped onto the rope with a clamp, which I could slide along, but which would lock onto the rope when I wanted it to. This section of slope seemed to be catching the wind at its strongest. Facing into the wind, I could not breathe, and I tried to make progress backwards. I could not keep my footing as the wind just blew me over. I went down on my knees, my head held low, and crawled up the slope. Constantly I was lifted from the ground, only to be stopped from being blown away by the rope, taut in the wind, singing under the tension.

The best method of movement was to rush and then rest. Fast movement is not easy at altitude, but movement was essential. I rested in a ball, face buried in arms, then rushed upwards for ten feet before collapsing, panting, in a crouch once more.

It was even more difficult where the ropes ran horizontally across the slope. Here I had to revert to moving backwards. The slope had steepened sufficiently to prevent me crouching in a ball and I could not face into the wind, nor could I move backwards at a rush. The force of the wind had reached a new peak and I seemed to be spending more time in mid air, like a kite, than on the surface of the snow. Even facing away from the wind it was difficult to breathe. A vacuum was formed on the side of my body in the lee of the wind, and I was panting furiously to overcome this unexpected suffocation. With my mouth thus gaping, ice started to form inside; the cold air I was sucking into my lungs was making them ache; my whole body was cold.

Panic started to take hold of me and I tried to reason that it was not too late to turn back. I felt dizzy and lethargic as the wind pushed me, first one way, then the other and I became completely disorientated. I knew my body heat was being whipped away every second. It seemed a silly place to die, just a few rope lengths away from the safety of the cave.

My fear increased and I heard my own voice saying: 'Come on, move!' The words came out as drunken slur. I recognized that. I had reached the point where the ropes crossed a six-foot-wide crevasse mostly concealed by snow – normally a place to avoid, but now it appeared as a friend. Still attached to the rope, I launched myself into its depths and an eerie calm set in. I was still panting and disorientated but the panic had been taken out of the moment. I had time to recover and consider whether to return to the ice cave or battle on to the rocks.

Half an hour later I poked my head out into the wind, which hit me like a wall of liquid. I went for the rocks, fighting every step with my body angled at 45° into the wind. I do not remember the final hundred feet along the rope, only the sense of relief as I collapsed in the lee of the rocks.

Pete arrived after a similar struggle and my spontaneous outbursts of terror and amazement were lost in the wind; but he did not need any descriptions from me.

Lower down, we came into snowfall, the once familiar route now disguised beneath a thickening blanket. Once easy ground was a nightmare of uncertainty; the ropes, sometimes buried deep in the snow, were swollen to three times their thickness with coatings of ice. We slipped and slid downwards for six hours, finally stumbling into Base Camp just in time for Christmas.

Brian had some criticisms about the route up to the West Shoulder. He felt that there had been a tendency by the twins and John to take the most obvious line, leaving Pete and himself to sort out the difficulties when the going became too hard. 'Let's think about it more carefully in future,' he said.

Opinions did differ, but the main obstacle was now overcome and it seemed good that this should have been achieved in time for Christmas and that we should all be down together to celebrate.

7 Christmas

The abnormal darkness for the time of the morning and, above my eyes, the sagging slopes of the tent from which there came the intermittent rustle of sliding snow, told me that the camp was still enveloped in the storm we had woken to the previous day. There would be no movement upwards today either, and aware now that we would all be seeing Christmas in together I was secretly relieved. It was not good to lose a single precious day of work on the mountain but now there was no option I could relax. The significance of Christmas now permeated my consciousness and I noted in my diary: 'An unreal situation – and at the same time so normal. All the residue of Christmases past, conviviality, warmth, presents, lights, friends, girlfriends, family – and here we are, here I am, waking to snowfall and grey, heavy weather at Base Camp. The bright spot being that we are all here and the mail runner should be back today, though weather was so bad yesterday that no plane would have come in, so it will be just mail from last week.'

All day was spent in lazy preparation for a Christmas feast. We had decided to have our party, American style, on the evening of Christmas Eve, since we were all together but, if the weather improved, three of us would be leaving to go up. Suddenly I realized how much it meant to me to celebrate Christmas and how eager I was for the mail runner to arrive.

John had miraculously preserved a small supply of drink – brandy, sherry and whisky – for this occasion and some decorations and ornamental lights, appeared. The dining tent took on a festive atmosphere as John, alternating between cook tent and dining tent, his face glowing more and more brightly, supervised events in the kitchen and helped himself to the chef's traditional tots of alcohol.

Five of the Japanese came over to join our celebrations. Uemura, storm-bound at Camp 2, sent us Christmas greetings, and our Sherpa staff caught the spirit of our enthusiasm, Wan Chup, for once, worked willingly under John's painstaking directions.

As darkness fell on a camp blanketed in snow, trays of delicacies were ferried across into the dining tent; dressed crab, smoked oysters, pate and more sherry. The constant roar of the wind from the Lho La was drowned by the cacophany of sound from our largest cassette deck which was thrust into the bottom of an empty, drumlike container to enhance the volume.

After a while the Japanese beamed their thanks, made their excuses with inscrutable politeness and left.

The main meal, chicken, stuffing, reconstituted powdered potato and dried vegetables, arrived and more whisky was found. John had kept his *pièce de résistance* a close secret and he produced it with a flourish, flaming Christmas pud and brandy sauce. I felt bloated and content. The one flaw in the day had been the failure of the, mail runner to arrive, perhaps on account of the snow.

By eight o'clock we were all laid out, drowsy and warm with the repletion of good food and drink. Stories were swapped and more banter passed around. Most of us were wearing our thick, red, down suits, making the tent seem like a gathering-place for Father Christmases. Ade, his nose a red glow, grinned mischievously and went off into a fantasy about job prospects: 'That must be a good number – being Father Christmas with all those girls that come to sit on your knee.' He and his brother now looked more alike than ever, since Ade had grown a rough beard and we relished the prospect of seeing again Al's girlfriend from Kathmandu, who had written to say she would meet us on the way back.

Only Paul and Alan remained talking. Sometimes one got the impression that Alan missed the complex, intellectual discussions of his Cambridge days. Often he, led the way in ribald humour, but underlying this was the suspicion of a keen intelligence which was yearning to be tested. Now Paul and Alan were locked in a discussion which centred round something about logarithmic equations inside a cube tending towards a point. Paul gave every appearance of holding his own, but to me it was totally incomprehensible and I gathered from the quizzical frown on Allen Jewhurst's face as he went off to bed that he was baffled too. I left as well and sank into a drunken sleep. Vague thoughts about the route, prompted by a starry sky, were lost in an alcoholic haze.

Perversely, the next day, Christmas Day, started fine and Paul, Alan and I made ready to go up to the Lho La. Just another work day for us and I envied those who remained their extra day of rest and celebration. It was 11 a.m. before we were ready to leave and the weather had changed. Clouds were blowing up from the south and streamers of snow were trailing off the ridge of Nuptse. There was every excuse to change plans and stay at Base but I was uncertain whether I was being influenced by common sense or the effects of the alcohol still lingering in my body. I left before delaying further and weakening. Paul and Alan, feeling no better, followed.

The well-known way up to the start of the ropes was transformed. Deep snow concealed all the familiar ledges and footholds, my hands became numb and gloves wet from the constant groping in the snow for holds. I dislodged a huge rock which lay buried and hidden, and blamed my impatience for getting ahead of the other two. I waited a long while but grew cold in the strengthening winds. I hurried on to warm up and started up the ropes of the overhanging groove without seeing Paul and Alan. From the halfway ledge I heard shouts and dimly through the swirling cloud made out a figure far below. It was difficult to hear against the noise of the wind, but it was Paul and I understood from him that he was turning back to Base Camp.

I reconsidered what I was doing. In less than an hour I would be at the snow cave; it would take longer to get back to Base Camp. I continued. The alcohol was probably still poisoning my system because the roar of the wind across the plateau above my head was like that heard inside a railway tunnel. Snow was falling thickly and it was no longer the fine day I had started, out on. We had all been lulled into a false estimation of the winter here by the relatively fine days we had experienced. I was inadequately clad, and urgently forced myself upwards before the cold penetrated to my bones. At the end of the rocks and start of the snow up and across to the cave I strapped on crampons, buffeted all the while by the Wind. I could not keep my footing and pulled, myself along on the slopes I had first crossed ten days ago, doubting then the necessity for fixing ropes. I reached the caves and escaped into the calmer recesses of the first one, feeling bruised, battered and exhausted. There was no sign of Alan behind me.

Pete and Brian had blocked the entrance with rucksacks but spindrift had forced its way in through every little crevice. Everything inside the cave, sleeping bags, clothes, food, was covered in a fine layer of snow. Someone's down suit was lying there so I slipped into it; mine was still over at the tent site and I did not want to venture back there. It took half an hour to clean the cave of snow, and after gathering a rucksack full of snow from outside I settled into a sleeping bag with a book.

At 6 p.m. I learnt from Ade on the radio that Alan had turned back too. Paul and Alan had both found they were going so slowly after the previous day's excesses that they were very cold and feared lest they should not reach the cave before dark. They had taken the safest course and retreated. I also learned that the mail runner had arrived. This completed my sense of isolation and loneliness.

'Is there any for me?' I asked hesitantly.

'Yes, I won't be able to bring any gear up tomorrow, my sack will be full of all your bloody letters. I haven't got any, I'm gonna open some of yours.'

After a few ribald comments Ade signed off. I crawled back into the cave, to spend Christmas evening on my own. I could sense a nostalgia in one part of me. I blocked it off, not thinking about who I might have letters from, forcing my thoughts into reading a rather predictable terrorist novel and made a meal, which was unenjoyable without someone to share it, last as long as possible.

The night on my own was a strange one. I blocked the cave entrance with rucksacks against the windblown snow that was billowing in. I had a suspicion that if I relaxed from a detached, unfeeling frame of mind, the bizarre nature of my situation – being alone at 20,000 feet on Everest, a mountain haunted by the ghosts of climbers dead on its slopes – might become disturbing. The cave was in sight of the spot where Mallory and Irvine had disappeared in 1924, and where their bodies may well still lie. I preferred to consider myself as being unaffected by superstition and I pushed out of my mind the sense of total loneliness which hovered on the fringes of my consciousness without the company of others to alleviate it. If I let such thoughts form and inner fears take hold, I felt they could possess and unbalance me. Sleep, once I had finished eating, came mercifully quickly and I was able to linger in an unthinking doze next morning until it was light, time to move and I could look forward to the arrival of more people and my post.

Four people arrived in the middle of the afternoon of Boxing Day – the twins, Paul and Alan – as I was finishing replacing some ropes which had become worn by the wind action rubbing them against the rock. I finished the work and joined them at the caves. I asked Ade for my mail. He looked startled and suddenly alarmed: 'I think our kid's got your letters.' He had not and I was filled with a welling resentment at their thoughtlessness. I was tempted to burst out with an attack on them for their lack of consideration but Ade looked crestfallen and was so full of self-criticism that I suppressed my annoyance. The twins are usually so thoughtful and considerate of others and they would censure themselves more heavily than I ever could, as they knew how highly prized letters are on a mountain. The fault really lay with us all, as we had no system by which messages and letters were automatically passed upwards, rather than left to the initiative of individuals.

In the morning the wind streamed strong and steady across the plateau between the, caves and the slopes up to the Western Shoulder. Paul and I were to go up and complete the route through the rock barrier. Al and Ade would carry loads in support, and Alan, feeling fully recovered now, was, going to make some necessary alterations to the caves.

It took half an hour, staggering in the wind, to cross the Lho La plateau. As I reached the opposite side the slope swept increasingly steeply, upwards to end at a gap in the ice, the bergschrund, ten feet wide, where the angle changed abruptly and a vertical wall of ice reared up on the other side. The crevasse was unfathomably deep and it was twenty feet up the vertical wall to where the angle eased off, but a rope was in place now, stretching across the gap, up the wall, and on up the slopes above. I clipped my ascendeur device onto the rope, slid it along and swung alarmingly across the bergschrund and up the wall to the slopes above.

The wind was coming from my right, the south. The hood of my down suit projected forward round my face like blinkers on a horse. Vision was severely restricted and the wind bounced off the snow and onto my face, icicles forming from my condensed breath on beard and moustache. A long repetition of movements upward was punctuated with frequent halts to regain my breath. I was panting hard, and I found I was having to face continually to the left to avoid the discomfort of icy blasts of wind against cheeks and nose.

I was impressed with the distance up to the rock barrier; the time taken, the gruelling slog up 1,500 feet of ropes, two and a half hours from the caves to a cluster of pitons, karabiners, and spare rope left by Brian and Pete at their high point. The difficulty of climbing the rock barrier was disguised for me now the ropes were in place, but I could see why it had taken a whole day for them to climb 300 feet and marvelled at the achievement. A slight anxiety and excitement gripped my stomach in anticipation of what we would have to face.

The ropes ended at a ledge on which I crouched against the wind, peering down at the others on the slope below. Time passed; I was sitting right in the path of the wind. I hunched myself up to present as small a target as possible; the cold ate into my bones.

It seemed like hours before Paul arrived; I was numb and useless. Paul too was chilled; his feet wooden and without feeling. Should we go on or not? I did not know if I would be steady enough to lead out on new ground. The wind had been too strong to move on without someone to safeguard me with a rope. Paul vacillated, but he too wondered about the wisdom of continuing in the state we were in.

I gave it a try. Movement restored some warmth and I was able to climb upwards on a runnel of ice partially sheltered from the wind. The exposed ledge I had left was probably the worst possible place to hang around. When I had the rope anchored to an 'ice screw', driven into the solid bank of ice up which I had climbed, Paul joined me. He had not been able to regain any warmth and Ade, close behind, volunteered to take his place.

The rock barrier far exceeded in difficulty anything we could see ahead. It was not easy ground by any means but there seemed no reason for us to reach an impasse here as we had done before.

I climbed up a band of brittle ice, my crampon points fracturing and splintering the surface before finding purchase. A wind formed ramp of snow led more easily to a slab of shattered rock into a crack in which I drove a piton. A little higher and I had reached the end of the rope. I led another 150 feet, legs straddling a shallow depression in the rock and crampons, awkward and insecure, scratching and sparking on the granite. Ade came up, tying off the rope at each anchor point I had placed and casting an appraising eye over my work. He was the only one amongst us with a guide's certificate and the lingering effects of his training still permeated his thinking.

I pressed him to lead for a while. It is much more exciting and satisfying to be out in front rather than humping a heavy load in support, though both are of equal importance. Ade unselfishly was not insisting on having a turn in front as he had done a good deal of the leading lower down. He did take over, though, and traversed diagonally rightwards up a sloping ledge of broken rocks, on and up over some black, insubstantial rock coated in ice. He made careful, measured progress for another 300 feet before the time was all eaten up and we had to descend.

Before we did, I clambered up a rib of rock for another forty feet to a vantage point from which to spy out the upper slopes. Ade followed and we were pleased to see that for the next 2,000 feet there were few obstacles comparable to the rock barrier.

We had overstayed our time limits. The sun sank behind the distant hills as we abseiled back down, casting rosy tints on the glistening ice through the rock barrier. It was dark before we wearily entered the snow caves.

Brian, Pete and John had come up earlier ferrying loads. I was surprised to find that John had not stayed, for we needed him to pair off with Al the next day so that the rest of us could have an easier day, taking our time, carrying loads in support. It seemed that there had been some dispute about movements. John had intended to stay up but Brian had insisted that there were enough people on the Lho La already, and John should stay below. There were five people at the Lho La but the work above was very demanding. The cold drained the energy and fatigue came on much more quickly than I had experienced before. The wind had a wearying effect, so it was better to keep a rotation going to replace people and distribute the work as much as possible. To have enough usable time in the day to break new ground and fix ropes we had to be up early and move fast up the already established route. Everyone else was too tired or due to descend, and I reluctantly faced the prospect of another's day exhausting work as now I would have to partner Al.

As Ade explained, this probably arose out of a discussion at Base Camp on Christmas Day. The subject had been raised about work distribution. In the absence of dictation from above, this was the democratic process at work. The twins and John were strongly of the opinion that some people were working much harder than others, whereas Pete and Brian were just as convinced that everyone had done about the same. Alan was convinced that everyone was working to his own personal limit, which was all that could be expected or was possible. Since no one wanted to establish a formal rota, clashes of opinion were inevitable.

Al and I did not do so much the next day. I was tired and left the cave late. It was not such easy ground as first thought and I found Al to be super-cautious, and his comments suggested that he found my methods to be on the careless side. Climbing back up to the previous day's high point, I was hard-pressed to keep up with his purposeful, steady pace. He followed the Diemberger theory that maintains that slow, no matter how slow, but constant movement is the best way to achieve progress at altitude. I could not stand the tedium of constant movement and when Al glanced back to see how I was doing I shouted up to him that I preferred 'interval training' – actually preferring the intervals to the training,

We ran out nearly 500 feet of rope and Paul and Alan toiled up as we finished for the day with heavy loads of rope and a tent. It was dark again before we regained the cave after a wild, sunset.

At last my mail had arrived. There was a card for Christmas from Maria showing a chorus line of eight buxom girls from the 'thirties, and the back of the card was smothered with the lipstick-imprinted shapes of different lips. Alan was disgusted that I could not tell which were Maria's. There was also a letter from my mother saying she was having a Mass said at Christmas for our safe return. This made a remarkable impression on everyone.

John was now here to stay, Brian and Pete were due to come up the next day, so Alan, Paul, Al and I descended. It was hard to sustain the energy to do anything effective for more than a couple of days without a rest and decent food. There was plenty of food in the caves but cooking a meal was a three-hour task and there was a tendency to miss out on eating and succumb to the constant feeling of lassitude induced by the altitude.

It was a stormy morning; the wind drove flurries of snow into the caves; John and Ade kept poking their heads out and trying to decide whether what to do. John wanted to go to find out what it was like to climb in really bad conditions. Ade, more cautious, did not want to waste a day battling upwards only to be driven back and be too tired to utilize the next day should it be fine.

I met Brian and Pete, coughs still troubling them, as I went down. The roar of the wind became more faint as I got lower and I felt with surprise the sun's warmth when it peeped through the clouds. The mountain was still wrapped in a swathe of cloud, still ravaged by the winds, a microcosm of turbulent weather all to itself.

In four nights I had become conditioned to accepting constant wind and cold. Base Camp was luxury by comparison. I revelled in the warmth of a sun that cast splendid light on the pinnacles and blocks of ice which reared up out of the glacier. A footpath had been trodden through the new snow that was painfully bright.

The mail runner had already left but I busied myself with writing cards and letters, an occupation made unpleasant by the cracks and sores in my fingers. The constant cold and necessity to handle rough objects lacerates the fingers and the cuts often turn septic. It was painful even to hold a pen. Graham, the sound man from the film crew, had slight frostbite in one of his fingers.

Of the three film-crew, Graham was the least certain about making this film. He was the quietest member of our whole group, often spending hours at a time without saying a word, soaking up with amazement the many tales of adventure and lawlessness which dominated conversations. After, one series of stories from which one could only deduce that the streets inhabited by the Burgess twins were pregnant with violence, Graham did interject a wry comment of 'Yes, I can't walk down a street in Harrogate without thinking someone's going to jump me from a doorway.'

On another occasion Al, after reading a book about a con-man who drugged and murdered his victims, questioned Pete about whether there was an antidote if one felt a strange drowsiness creeping over one and suspected poison. Al saw such knowledge as relevant to his own life-style. Graham parodied him with a bubbling smile: 'Is there anything you can take, Pete, if you feel the point of a knife in your back? Anything to stop that taking effect?'

Graham had gone up onto the lower slopes with Allen and Mike to do some filming and sound recording. For the climbers, being filmed made little difference except that it took longer to get from one place to another as we were often asked to repeat a section so that it could be filmed from a different angle. The film crew were static for most of the time and even when the sun was out the actual air temperature was still well below zero. Only movement kept one warm. One day Graham's feet and hands were numb without him realizing it. Once numb, they can freeze solid without one knowing. It is only while one feels the cold that one knows there is still blood circulating and sensation still there.

Without knowledge of all these details Graham was not aware of anything except that he was more clumsy at handling things and it was only on returning to Base, where his hands and feet thawed out and pain came with the returning sensation as the blood tried to revive the dying tissue, that he realized his toes were 'frost-nipped', that is in the first stages of frostbite, and he spent many hours standing up, stamping his feet up and down to induce warmth and clasping his hands in his armpits. Graham found he could hardly eat any of the food, just the smell of it revolting him. This was a feature of living at altitude and is not uncommon. He seemed to shrink visibly before our eyes and having weighed himself on some scales at the Japanese camp found that he had lost two stones in weight.

During these days a visitor arrived, an Australian who had braving the rigours of winter came up to Base Camp, relying upon us to feed and shelter him. It is part of the agreeable spirit of the mountains that such hospitality should be shown, but I did feel he took too much for granted and found that I resented the intrusion into our private world as much as if I walked into my house to find a complete stranger making himself at home and asking questions about my private affairs. I realized that I had come to terms completely with our life in the mountains and felt like an animal in a zoo when anyone came to stare and probe with questions.

He did, however, bring disturbing news. He had been at Lobuje and seen our mail runner offering for money to the Sherpani who ran the tea house, wind kept grabbing at the tent; I tried and failed many times to locate the poles in the necessary places. Paul held on but I was the only one who had used these tents, had sung their praises and now could not expect more than minimal help as the method of erecting it was too complicated to be passed on when every, shouted word was snatched away , by the wind. I bent one of the aluminium tubes into place to form an arc from which the tent would hang. The pole snapped, I felt a fool for advocating the use of this tent. The weather on K2 had been terrible, but the quality of the cold on Everest was much more severe. My useless hands fumbled with other poles as I tried various ways of botching up my blunder. Paul watched with mute, helpless interest. With the poles finally in place I suspended the light inner tent from the arcs formed and turned to pulling the orange outer tent over the framework. It is the outer tent which gives the structure strength. When properly in place the arcs hold the outer skin in tension and a stable dome is formed. The last manoeuvre of pulling the outer tent over the end of the pole is hardest and in my struggles, with the tent lifting in the air, another pole snapped. I was furious but allowed my fury to rage without stopping my movements for a moment. Brian appeared, dropped his load, and grabbed the tent too.

It was not a perfect job, but when we had finished the tent was upright and, for the moment, withstanding the wind. We drove stakes into the snow to anchor the tent and buried the edges with blocks of ice and more snow. I dived inside, Paul scuttled off to his own tent and Brian hurried back down to Camp 1. These slopes were no place to linger needlessly, and tears were already forming in my eyes at the pain of frozen fingers returning to life.

Alan arrived late in the afternoon and settled into the tent with me. The icy platform beneath the ground sheet was uneven, and near the edge it was insubstantial. The useable floor space of an already tiny tent was much reduced. We both shuffled into sleeping bags and, pressed close against each other, tried to impose some sort of order onto the chaos of food and gear strewn inside the tent. If it was not done before dark we would have no hope of locating anything we needed.

An icy layer began to form on the inside surface of the tent fabric as the condensation from our breathing came into contact with the cold material and froze. It was 5 p.m. and almost dark before we were reclining in uncomfortable readiness to prepare the evening meal. Suddenly we heard the slow, rhythmic crunch of footsteps outside and the sound of Pete coughing; he had just arrived.

'Pete, it will be dark soon, what are you doing up here?'

He had set off with a load, as we knew, but, instead of descending in time to regain Camp 1 before dark, had continued. There was no sleeping bag for him and no room. He had on his down suit, the normal clothing up here, but it was so cold that a sleeping bag as well was necessary to survive the night.

'Oh, I'll be all right.'

He seemed unconcerned and passed by to visit Al and Paul at the other tent. I was amazed when he did not leave for another half hour. There were ropes all the way down to the level plateau of the Lho La but in the dark it is so easy to make a fatal mistake.

'Have you got a torch?'

'Yeah, I'll be all right,' he repeated and crunched off Alan looked at me with incomprehension and shook his head.

The tent we were in differed from the box tent occupied by Al and Paul in that there was an inner tent and outer shell. The outer shell came right down to floor level and had a flap on which we had placed blocks of ice and snow. We could thus open the doors on the inner tent without the wind blowing in. This enabled us to collect snow to melt and allowed us to ventilate the tent whilst cooking.

Hoar-frost formed a thickening layer on every surface; a dangling piece of nylon cord grew to three times its usual size with the accumulation of ice crystals on it. Outside the wind swept ceaselessly across the ice slope into which we had cut a slot for the tent.

Each gust which shook the tent sent down showers of ice, and undermined any confidence in it surviving the night. One of us had to be attentive to the stove the whole time to prevent it overturning and soaking clothes and food. It was a wretched, squalid scene.

I was too uncomfortable to sleep easily and the noise from the wind banging at the tent kept me in a state of nervous anticipation. The box tent was twenty feet below but communication was impossible. Alan has the enviable ability of relaxing and sleeping in the most painful circumstances, an accomplishment which he attributes to his drunken youth at Cambridge when he frequently spent the night where he fell. I needed a sleeping pill to block out the discomfort and anxiety.

The whole of the next day was spent enlarging the tent platform and building a protective wall of snow blocks as a wind break. There was no let up in the ferocious buffeting of the wind and stinging snow flurries; no opportunity for consultation; each person did what he thought best. Al felt ill after two successive nights of disturbed sleep and insufficient food. He shuffled off down.

Our purpose in being at Camp 2 was to continue upwards but until we had a comfortable camp we could do little and against this wind there was no hope of progress. All efforts were focused on merely surviving the savage, inescapable cold. The tents seemed like flies against the massive wind which battered the mountain. I was incapable of undressing sufficiently to relieve myself, the cold was so severe.

In the midst of another wretched night I awoke in terror feeling snow on my face and in the bewilderment between nightmare and wakefulness shook

Alan and asked if he was alright. It was the recurring nightmare which had troubled me ever since the avalanche high on K2. The sensation I had experienced on waking to find snow pouring remorselessly down and crushing me under a black, soundless blanket before losing consciousness, had left a lasting mark on my psyche.

Alan reassured me that nothing had changed. The tent was still shaking in the wind and a torch, shone inside, showed the constant showers of hoar-frost which fell from a layer a quarter-inch thick which covered the walls and roof. Alan had a rough night which left him listless and weary next day. He descended to Camp 1 to escape for a while from the horror of life at Camp 2. Paul came by a little later. He too felt dreadful after a third night spent in the path of the winds. Even though the wind did not penetrate the tents, the noise wore on the nerves and there was the ever-present anxiety that the fabric of the tent would tear or the poles would break. Inside the tents the air temperature varied -30 degrees Celsius and -40 degrees Celsius. A stove did not seem to make any difference, we had to wear gloves the whole time, and rather than raise the temperature a stove only increased the depth of hoar-frost which formed inside the tent.

I shared a drink I had ready with Paul, who described the discomfort of the box tent before descending to the secure caves of Camp 1, and I was left alone.

Alone again on this hostile mountain. I wrote in my diary, which had become little more than a series of notes to mark the passage of time: 'On most mountains there is some respite; once on the Lho La there is a constant battering of the psyche and body by the wind and cold. It really is grim waking up here to a tent coated with rime.'

A weak sun made a pale appearance through the clouds but the rime never left the tent all day. I wondered what I could do. Camp 2 was at 22,500 feet; I considered going on my own to survey the ground above or dropping back to bring up some rope and equipment which had accumulated at various points on the way. Being left alone took the urgency out of doing anything, and since each time I opened the tent door a swirling cloud of snow blew in, I let the day slip away completely without stirring outside.

There was no radio at Camp 2 and no means of guessing the movements of anyone else. The cold and altitude had a numbing effect on my sensitivity as well as my flesh. I did not stir from my sleeping bag all day, welcoming the extra space now that Alan had gone, and drifted periodically in and out of sleep, like someone in a hospital bed. No one else arrived that day and as dark came on I prepared a solitary meal which I ate as a duty.

I took two sleeping pills to wipe out my stark surroundings but was woken at 10 p.m. by the crash of wind against the tent. I lay for the rest of the night listening and worrying whether the tent would hold. Morning was welcome for the arrival of light but the wind did not lessen; I was too fatigued to make any progress outside, and reluctant to undergo the chore of stowing all the gear strewn inside the tent and face the unpleasantness of descending to Camp 1.

I can no longer remember the experience of being alone; I find it hard to comprehend that I spent three days without stirring above the tent at Camp 2. Like the gum anaesthetized by the dentist's needle, insensitive but not dead, I performed the minimum necessary to survive but languished in comatose inactivity whenever possible. Three days and no possibility, no thought of upward movement. I did not miss the company of others but noticed the passage of time in which I had not said a word. Sometimes I did think aloud but cut off any philosophical musings which probed the sense of what I was doing.

By early afternoon, having glimpsed the mental lassitude, which can induce the physical paralysis leading to death, I had resolved to escape downwards. I packed gear into rucksacks which I placed outside into a maelstrom of snow, found the lifeline of rope, and headed down. My legs, unaccustomed after my confinement to exercise, collapsed under me as I slid down the ropes and my hands fumbled weakly at each knot. When I reached the level plateau of the Lho La, standing freely for the first time in days, I dropped one of my ascendeurs which slid down a slight incline for fifty feet. I was too tired to go after it. Stumbling and falling, I made my way back against the wind to the snow caves.

Innumerable accidents occur when people become separated or isolated on a mountain. In the prevailing wild weather, Paul and Alan were anxious lest I should try to fight my way down alone or remain trapped for days if no one else could get up.

'It's all right leaving someone on his own if you want an exciting story to take back,' said Alan, 'but not if you want to climb a mountain safely.'

I relaxed into the security of the cave as Alan prepared endless drinks and food, which he passed over to Paul and me. We had done no more than spend a few days at 22,500 feet but we felt as if we had survived a traumatic ordeal and could luxuriate in the relative comfort of this Camp 1 cave. The temperature inside was -10 degrees Celsius.

Later in the afternoon John arrived and the sight of the three of us languishing in sleeping bags brought on a torrent of recrimination from him. He was highly critical of the lack of progress above Camp 2, and censorious of the amount of food we were consuming whilst lying inactive at Camp I.

With the slow deliberation of the self-righteous I explained to him the conditions we had experienced, and gradually it sank into John that the sunny days he had been enjoying at Base Camp bore no relation to the brutal life on the mountain. Contrite and apologetic, John agreed that he was 'sounding off a bit' without sufficient awareness of our situation.

Ade was also meant to be coming up with Mike, the cameraman; John had last seen them doing some filming in the overhanging groove. Mike had done some rock climbing in Britain but even though we had ropes in place all the way to the cave now we preferred that one of us should be with him on the mountain as much as possible. The amount of camera equipment that was accumulating at the Lho La was alarming; it clearly showed the differences of emphasis between the climbers and the film crew. I felt strongly that not a single day should be lost in climbing the mountain through attention to the film.

By dark the fierce winds still ripped across the slopes outside and there was no sign of Ade and Mike. The never distant unease surfaced. I left the warmth of my sleeping bag, fastened on my harness and crawled out into the, night. I could not stand in the wind. I clipped some ascenders to the anchored rope and pulled myself up the incline. After 100 feet the ropes crossed the slope horizontally but still I could not stand. I crawled on all fours, my harness fastened to the rope by the ascender which allowed me to pull myself forward without sliding back. I couldn't see in the dark, I couldn't look up into the wind without my face being stung with snow and numbing instantly. It was only 300 feet to the rocks at the far side and three times I was picked up and thrown up the slope by the force of the wind. I felt idiotic and presumptuous against such power. I descended to the top rim of the amphitheatre and peered into the dark; no sight, no sound above the wind. I shouted uselessly and turned back.

At the far side of the traverse across the slope a shadowy figure, cowled and ominous, stood waiting. It was Paul, his back to the wind, waiting to make sure I was safe. No word passed, we descended to the cave and in the calm inside I told them. I had found nothing.

A radio call at 6 p.m. to Base Camp revealed that they had not arrived back. We arranged a recall at 7 p.m. and with relief heard that Ade and Mike had appeared ten minutes earlier. I always have a slight sense of foolishness as if I have been over-reacting in such situations, but to wait until one is sure that something has gone wrong is to invite tragedy.

We spent a restless night; the roof of the cave seemed to lift with the force of the wind, ear drums popped with the sudden pressure changes as the wind hammered at the entrance, the thump of the blasts kept everyone's nerves on edge.

Morning brought no change. We concocted a meal from freeze-dried scrambled egg mixed with chunks of tinned ham. It tasted almost like real food.

By 1 p.m. we were too tired and dispirited to stay up any longer. The weather showed no signs of improvement and I radioed down our decision.

Once at the top of the corner I slid down away from the constant roar which had been with me for days – it was like a climatic deconditioning process. A thousand feet lower and a parting in the clouds let sunlight filter through and warm my body and I began to relax and the tension of the last few days ebbed away. These walls of rock which had taken all our efforts were now reassuring and pleasant to pass over. I realized that I had not relieved myself for three days and a sudden overwhelming urge forced me to rip open my harness, down suit and underclothes to release three days of constipation just in time.

9 'In the mountains one forgets to count the days'

There was a poor bag of mail waiting for us. Alan fretted at the continued lack of letters from his girlfriend. I tried to reassure or commiserate with him since: I had not had a letter from Maria for three weeks, nor from my mother, who writes dutifully every Sunday. My attempt at reassurance had the opposite effect. Alan just thought I was more inhuman and unfeeling than him. On expeditions I had come to make a deliberate point of not letting emotional events affect me. I feel the lack of letters deeply but to worry about what might or might not be happening in another way of life is to conjure up a punishing fantasy world which can disturb one's thoughts and influence one's decisions. For many years whilst I trained to be a Catholic priest I lived in a dream world, planning for the holidays when I could really live, escaping mentally from the strait-jacket of a rigid timetable, strict rules and enforced behaviour. Having left that regime, I had an antipathy towards any tendency to live in fantasy worlds, preferring to think only about what I knew I could do and not to live in hope only to be disappointed or to find that the reality did not live up to my dreams.

On an expedition I exercised a possibly harmful capacity for viewing situations and events from my other life in a detached, anaesthetized manner. Of late, expeditions had gone on for a long time and on returning to England I found it took me quite a while before I regained the habit of feeling and emotion. This was very difficult for anyone close to me.

The heavy snows we were experiencing were affecting flights to Syangboche; from where our mail was collected. This was one reason for the small offering brought by the mail runner.

A party of eight Italians had arrived and made a Base Camp near ours. They were intending to climb Lhotse, the fourth highest mountain in the world, by the route which had defeated the Poles in 1974/75. They were a jolly bunch, a little disconcerted by the rigours of winter and concerned that their clothing was not adequate. They brought a comment from Reinhold Messner, who had climbed Everest twice without oxygen, and who is regarded as something of a god in Italy. He considered it impossible to climb the mountain in winter without oxygen.

I believed that he would have produced a different opinion if he had set his mind to attempting just that. Part of the reason for our being on Everest in winter was to find out what was possible.

It was true that some discouragement prevailed in our camp. The long spells of fine weather from December were gone, and any forecast picked up on Radio Nepal only spoke of winds of 100 knots, sometimes 120 knots, precipitation and cloud. The forecasts were of little help. In contrast to other seasons, the weather seemed to change radically in a very short space of time and without warning. The Japanese expedition was also having difficulty contending with the unpredictable arrival of sudden snow storms.

Life was comparatively easy physically at Base Camp and mentally relaxing for me with the knowledge that for the moment I was due a rest. A book I was reading, written in the style of Hemingway, about the Caribbean, sub-aqua escapades and cocktails on hotel verandas at sunset contrasted dreamily with our spartan existence. I missed a radio call one morning because I had left the set outside my sleeping bag and the batteries were cold. Normally I slept with the radio close to my body to keep it operable. My camera too had to be kept in my sleeping bag and I often dropped off to sleep in the escapist cocoon of sound on the headphones of my a tiny Sony cassette deck, which was also pushed down into the warmth.

From Base Camp I could see through the powerful telephoto lens that the tents at Camp 2 were still in place, but on the radio we learnt that no one had yet moved up there. A whole day had been spent assisting Mike with his loads of film equipment up to the Lho La and more gear had still to be collected from where it had been dumped. This was just what we had been wary of, having to spend valuable time shepherding one of the film crew up or down the mountain. There was a clear conflict of interests between the demands of the film and the needs of the climb. Lost days were irreplaceable and although, we could not reasonably leave any of the film crew to move about on their own on any difficult sections this had to be the last time that efforts to climb the mountain were distracted by the film. I felt an infuriating annoyance at what seemed to be such an obvious mistake in priorities.

Al and I planned to go back up the next day, 10 January. Paul and Alan were afflicted by a return of the dysentery which had lingered round our camp and needed a little more rest.

Life at Base Camp had settled into a routine. There were no more problems with the staff except that the food did not have the same variety or taste as it had had during the approach march. The cook was battling against adverse circumstances in trying to produce palatable food on the temperamental stoves. Even the custard which was produced was uncooked or burnt. We summoned Mingma, the cook boy, to complain, as custard is the easiest thing in the world to make. He did not seem well suited to have his efforts rejected. With bad grace he took back the custard, taking a flying kick at some broken stoves which lay outside.

Al kept us entertained with another story of bewildered involvement in violence from an occasion when he and his brother, on a rare visit home, had taken their mother out for a meal. On leaving the restaurant to drive home they found that someone had broken into the car and was sitting in the driver's seat ready to drive off. As he described it I could visualize the two of them moving into action as in a scene from a gangster movie.

'I was a bit worried about what to do,' said Al.

'Why? Were you frightened?'

'No, it's just that you never know what your mother is going to think, do you? We just roughed him up a little bit.'

On the return to Camp 1 for once I was moving faster than Al, but I suspected that he had a heavier load than me. To gain the slopes leading up to where we had ropes in place we had to cross beneath the threatening walls of ice hanging below the Lho La. It only took fifteen to twenty minutes to pass over the exposed area and there were two schools of thought about the best line to take. In 1978 I had seen a monumental avalanche from the. Lho La. All seemed quiet in winter but I chose to take an indirect line that entailed an uncomfortable scramble for a long way up the unstable rocks skirting the glacier. The Burgess twins, exponents of fitness and speed, took a line for as far as possible up a gully directly in the fall line from the ice walls. They maintained that they could run to one side out of the way of anything falling. We came to call their way the 'Burgess couloir'. I told them that I would rather take ten minutes longer to get up the mountain than present the slightest opportunity of being caught in an avalanche. The other members of the team oscillated between the two schools of thought.

It was not unusual for me to part amicably from other people and wend a separate way up to where we picked up crash helmets and harnesses to start the more difficult climbing.

Mike Shrimpton was in residence at the caves filming our approach and clearly awed by his surroundings. Ade and John, Pete and Brian had gone on up to Camp 2 that day.

For the rest of the afternoon we lay inside the cave in sleeping bags, discussing the route, the film and climbing in general. Mike questioned us on our ideas for a title for the film. 'How about "Everest – Another Pawn in the Game"?' He was trying to locate the significance of trying to climb Everest by even harder, ever different routes, and our reasons for doing it. I did not think it was a very compelling title, nor that it did justice to the continual development of climbing exploring of the frontiers of the possible.

Al and I promised to rendezvous with Mike next day in the afternoon when the light was good as we descended from carrying loads up to Camp 2. We intended to reclimb the rock barrier so that Mike could film it. Mike had begun to appreciate some of the problems we had raised when he was proposing the film equipment he would like on the mountain. He had the biggest movie camera I had ever seen outside of picture books as it was and he was still not satisfied with the tripod I had carried up with great effort.

Mike was a real professional. As the expedition had gone on I had acquired an increasing respect for his energy and thoroughness in tackling his job. The television industry is hamstrung by union regulations and conditions and sometimes I wondered how Mike came to terms with the subconscious demands this background made on him. There was no conceivable way in money terms that anyone could be compensated for putting up with the conditions on Everest in winter. We had had problems in the first place owing to union rules that stated we should take along an electrician whose job is to set up and plug in the lighting. The fact that there was no electric power source on Everest carried no weight and the thousands of extra pounds which a surplus film crew member would entail resulted in our making the film as an independent enterprise.

Mike was on Everest because he wanted to be there, and the breadth of his experience as cameraman on 'Whicker's World', Arthur C. Clarke's 'Mysterious World' and many other assignments which had taken him to most countries in the world gave him a maturity and broad-minded vision which was an asset to the team as a whole.

The next day we were planning would be a demanding and exhausting one but if successful would mean that a major part of Mike's filming programme on the mountain was completed. Thereafter smaller cameras handled by the climbers were to be used. We, talked late into the night before snuggling down into sleep.

We were woken in the middle of the night by the unnerving thump of the wind driving, in powerful gusts, into the snow cave entrance; the increase in pressure made our ear drums, pop, and thereafter I was awake for the rest of the night, vaguely aware of the restlessness of Al and Mike, lying listening to the frightening roar of the wind outside. The thump of the wind and subsequent pressure waves were as I imagined it to be in a bunker under mortar attack. We were quite secure, in my mind I knew, but the four others had gone up and were occupying the fragile tents of Camp 2. I could not imagine the tents surviving such winds. Anxiously we awaited the radio call at 7 a.m.

I crouched in the entrance of the cave, buffeted by a wind which seemed to have concrete solidity, holding onto an axe driven into the ice as I called up Camp 2 on the radio. No reply. Every half hour I opened up the radio, hoping for some sign that the four at Camp 2 were alive. At eight thirty the radio crackled in reply. Ade was saying something about a tent being destroyed in the wind then the message came to a strangled end. Uneasily I conveyed the news to Al and Mike and periodically we crawled along the tunnel entrance to peer at the slopes of ice, glimpsed through swirling cloud, waiting for a sight of figures descending and the relief that this would bring.

At 10 a.m. I saw a figure through a telephoto lens moving hurriedly downwards. Ade arrived, instantly reassuring us that no accident had happened, and John followed some time later. All were safe but the collapse of the tent had thrown John and Ade on the mercy of the wind. John's hands had frozen solid and, near fainting with pain from the cold, he had pushed himself into the cramped confines of the still standing box tent where Brian and Pete had a pan of tea heating. John thrust his hands into the hot liquid and gradually the circulation returned.

Ade reckoned that the box tent would stand against the wind but Brian and Pete were finding life quite miserable inside. Every gust of wind showered them with the ice which lined the tent. He did not know whether they planned to stay up at Camp 2.

Disconsolate and bewildered, we retired to our sleeping bags and lay all day listening to the howling wind outside, feeling the thud of impact when it drove into the entrance.

Brian and Pete appeared out of the swirling mist towards late afternoon and occupied the other cave with John. Morale was at a low ebb and progress against such savage, elemental fury seemed impossible.

Ade explained that the wind had somehow got underneath the tent, lifted it up and snapped the poles. Fortunately this had happened at 6 a.m., just before dawn. The chaos of such an event in the full dark of night was too frightening to contemplate.

Ade was tired; we fed him drinks and food, and he dozed on and off. In the course of the afternoon we discussed our chances on the mountain. Ade was of the opinion that we had no hope of making any significant progress from the tents. Even if they withstood the wind it was not possible to rest well enough to do a day's work. Spending a night in the tent took all one's energy. He suggested a snow cave as the only possible solution.

Time seemed to be running out on us. Camp 2 had first been reached eleven days before and since then all eight of us had spent some time in the tents without moving any further up the mountain. I suggested siting a cave 1,000 feet higher where the slopes eased off before the final crest of the shoulder. I had come round to accepting a point of view I had been against earlier because of the effort involved. Al and I agreed to go up, put up with the discomfort of the box tent, and work regardless of the weakening effects of the altitude and discomfort until there was some semblance of a cave for the next party to occupy. We would have to descend after this as, even if all went well, we would be exhausted after such sustained work, but it presented the only chance of establishing a secure foothold high on the mountain. With a cave higher than the tent site we hoped to avoid placing another camp before 25,000 feet, thus cutting down on some of the time and effort. It seemed a logical proposal.

The two caves of Camp 1 were connected by a window hole, but because of the draught which streamed through we kept the hole blocked with a rucksack and spare clothes. Thus without thinking we had come to a conclusion without involving John, Brian and Pete. Next morning, as Ade left to go down for a rest, since now there was only room for two people at Camp 2, and he wanted to be ready to take over once the cave was dug, he poked his head into the other cave and found complete disagreement with the proposal. It seemed so logical a solution to an impasse we had now battled against for almost a fortnight that I had assumed it was in everyone's minds.

All three in the cave next door felt it was too risky to place all our hopes on finding a place suitable for digging a cave on ground no one had yet reached. Their proposal was to dig a cave at the site of Camp 2. Arguments in favour of both points of view were pushed back and forth. Nothing was lost, the bitter weather precluded any movement for a time anyway. A compromise was reached. Al and I would continue with our plan but the other three would also come up and start to dig a cave near the tents as a fall back position should the first plan prove over-ambitious. They could not stay up at Camp 2, but would dig for as long as possible before returning to Camp 1.

Next day I woke early and looked out of the cave at dawn. The sky was clear and the wind less strong. A bank of cloud low in the sky to the south seemed far enough away to present no immediate threat. We breakfasted, fastened on crampons and harness and prepared to go. The bank of cloud now filled the sky completely to the south, the front edge already catching the West Shoulder, and Nuptse's summit poured forth its own stream. Al and I looked at each other undecided and annoyed. I felt as if the mountain, like an anonymous, perverse bureaucracy, was treating us, without feeling.

From the confines of their cave, Brian said he thought we should go up and Pete echoed his opinion. Their tunnelled view revealed only blue skies. Even on seeing the advancing cloud Pete was forthright in his insistence that we should go up: 'It doesn't matter if you go up and the weather turns bad. If you get worn out again at Camp 2 there are plenty of other people to replace you.'

Even had I agreed with his philosophy I resented being pushed like this into an action of which I was uncertain. Al and I wandered down away from the cave, down the upper slopes of the Rongbuk glacier into China. We wanted to wait an hour to see if the weather improved and also to gain a view of the summit which, from the caves, of Camp 1, was hidden by the Western Shoulder. The slopes formed a gentle descent for half a mile before breaking up into crevasses and becoming a convoluted mass of ice towers and pinnacles where the glacier changed direction.

Across the glacier basin from where we stood we could clearly see the North Ridge, scene of many of the early attempts to climb Everest, and lost somewhere in the ice-coated immensity of the upper slopes of the mountain were the bodies of Mallory and Irvine. I felt very much the novice gazing on history. From the head of the basin rose a fine line of snow bisecting the rock of the North Face. Somewhere in that region Sherpa Ang Phu had died when he slipped whilst descending during the Yugoslav expedition to the West Ridge in 1979.

Above our Camp 2 on the West Ridge we could see that the slopes eased back and a thousand feet above the camp there was a hollow in the snow which gave hope of a possible site for a cave.

We returned to the caves of Camp 1 to find Brian retching outside. In the relentless cold of the winter he had no hope of recovering if he stayed on the mountain. He and John descended to Base Camp.

That evening on the radio Ade called us up and let us know that one member of the Japanese team had been killed when he slipped from the ice slopes below their Camp 3 on the other side of the mountain. I did not know the man in question; he was as anonymous as any fatality mentioned in a news bulletin. I felt no sense of loss as at the death of a friend, but a sickening sense of the futility of this whole enterprise of climbing, the inherent folly of the pursuit, pervaded my thoughts. We settled down to sleep that night talking about our roles as pawns in a game of our own choosing.

Al, Pete and I left next day in similar weather to that which had made us uncertain about starting the day before. The wind streamed steadily across the plateau and the slopes up to Camp 2. I was surprised to recognize in the crisp surface of the snow the marks of my crampons from the last time I had been up. My crampons were, completely different from anyone else's, having a distinctive rectangular shape. In spite of all the snow which had fallen, the constant action of the wind had swept the slopes clear, preserving the imprint. At any other season more snow may fall, but the temperature is higher, the snow contains more moisture and adheres more readily to a surface, and above all the wind is neither so fierce nor so constant. I was ahead of the other two and saw one figure turn back from the start of the ropes. At Camp 2 I spent some time clearing the tent of snow, making it ready for a late return. If our plan was to work we would be climbing till nightfall and would want to just tumble into our sleeping bags on our return. Much snow had infiltrated the tent during the events surrounding the stormy evacuation of a couple of days ago. Twenty feet above the box tent lay the sad wreckage of the tent I had spent three nights in some long time ago. The platform we had laboured so hard to dig was still there, partly covered in drifted snow, through which poked tent material, abandoned rucksacks and broken tent poles.

Suddenly Pete came into view, rising over the shoulder of rock above the tents and dropping down. I had assumed it to be Al who was coming up. Pete explained that the wind had chilled Al to the point where he was worried he was getting frostbite. The prospect of five hours pulling upwards on ropes in the same wind caused him to turn back and descend to Base Camp. It was more than just feeling chilly. By this time we had been at Base Camp or above for five weeks and the punishing effect of living in such extreme cold was taking its toll. Sometimes it was too difficult to force down the unappetizing food on the mountain and even at Base Camp the meals seemed to be less and less palatable. Without a big daily intake of food it was impossible to keep warm.

Al's absence was a blow. I regarded the twins as the strongest and fittest of us all, so for Al to go down was psychologically very discomforting. Pete and I made ready to climb, neither of us really knowing each other, and with that detailed politeness which characterizes the interaction of strangers, we agreed upon a way of tackling the wind-scoured slopes above.

The uncertain weather of early morning had changed unnoticed into an afternoon of blue skies, sun and only light wind. I led off The climbing was not difficult but troubled by slabs of loose snow adhering uncertainly to the underlying firmer surface I skirted round these slabs, fearing lest they give way and the accumulated might of a vast area should transform the insubstantial patches into an overwhelming, deadly wave. I led for 300 feet, stopping frequently to rest and, when Pete took over, relaxed in the enjoyment of a rare, fine day. For the first time I was actually enjoying being on the mountain; the view north into the brown, mysterious land of Tibet, the receding rows of hills to north and south, their contours etched more beautifully by the sinking sun, all filled me with a suppressed sense of privilege and, exaltation. Unfortunately it was an enjoyment I could not share, for Pete was far above me. Much of climbing on a big mountain is solitary, many hours are passed in the sole company of one's own shadow, other people separated by distance or weather from communication.

I wanted the afternoon to go on and on. I wished that everyone else could share the experience, for this if anything would revive the flagging spirit of the expedition.

When Pete had fixed 300 feet of rope in place I took another turn and took a false line up a runnel of snow beside an area of glassy ice. Pete corrected the error by traversing beneath the ice, and we lost some time in sorting out the ropes. He disappeared round a ridge of snow, and when the rope stopped moving I followed.

Nothing prepared me for what I saw when I came round the ridge. My attention was on the rope and on my crampons trying to find purchase on an icy passage. The slope had eased back completely now and I was almost walking. Looking up I was halted by the towering sight of the, summit pyramid of Everest, looming up so close, reddening in the setting sun which threw into relief all the cracks and wrinkles of this ageless mountain. I looked and looked as the colours changed, the red deepened, and dark shadow crept inexorably upward finally to wipe all colour away Pete shared his thoughts with a brief:

'Great isn't it?' and we made ready to return to Camp 2, well pleased with the day.

The unexpected sight made such an impression on me that I slid down the ropes, bubbling with eagerness to radio down the news of our progress. I tried a call at 5.30 p.m. before reaching the Camp but had no success and my numb, clumsy hands, cramped by the post-sunset chill, made me fear to use the radio lest I dropped it. It was a mere half hour back to the tent compared with the whole afternoon we had spent climbing upwards.

When we did make contact at the pre-arranged fallback time of 6 p.m. I transmitted the satisfaction both of us felt at breaking through the impasse we had reached at Camp 2 and our enthusiasm inspired by the sight we had seen. Ade, at Base Camp, was surprised. They had had a cold, windy day below and had expected us to fare worse. He promised to come up next day with Paul and Alan.

The satisfaction at the day's work and the conviction that we would be able to get a snow cave above helped us face the prospect of a grim night in the coffin of a tent which remained standing at Camp 2. The box tent was only just big enough for two of us. No movement could be made without the coopera-tion of the other person. Pete drew himself up into a corner of the tent to make room for me to cook. I had explained to him the great disinclination I feel to wake up on a morning and that if it suited him I would cook all the evening meal if he would cook the breakfast. Since there was only room for one person to cook at a time this made a logical division of work. For the next three hours I melted snow, made a stew, made drinks and passed them over.

'I'm glad you like plenty to drink,' said Pete. I was with Brian and he pre-ferred to go to sleep rather than eat and drink.' Pete was acquiring a reputation for being a big eater, maintaining a capacity to funnel food down endlessly. On an expedition it is an admirable accomplishment as normally everyone loses weight due to the loss of appetite, with the consequent diminishment of strength and stamina. In spite of the value of being able to continue eating, Pete's ability to do so did arouse a sense of annoyance and envy. It was irra-tional, but part of the inevitable dynamics of a living situation where comfort is at a minimum and sensitivity close to the surface.

It was so uncomfortable in the tent that there was little hope of dropping off to sleep. We each took a sedative and dozed fitfully. I was half aware of Pete being restless and muffled groans escaped from him each time he moved. At midnight I did not feel as if I had slept at all and when I spoke to Pete he said he could not sleep either because of some pains in his side. We took a sleeping pill each and I took two headache tablets. It was a heavy dosage and I woke at dawn dazed and groggy. Pete, unaccountably, was wide awake. He prepared breakfast and I trailed unenthusiastically after him to the top of the ropes, our high point of the previous day.

There was no need to fix rope as ground we had reached as it was only gently sloping, and the weather had remained unusually calm for a second day. We did run out some rope, however, until we arrived at a bank of snow in which we intended to dig a snow cave. Without the guideline of a rope it could be impossible to find the cave in a blizzard or hold on against a wind.

My head had cleared of its earlier muzziness. Pete, smaller than me but more stocky, disguised in a. similar spaceman's garb of quilted red suit, plodded up steadily. He had a purposeful pace; I projected onto him the assumption that he was unaffected by the debility which I felt. Even walking close together little was said, I was panting hard and any comment I made sounded as if I attached great weight to it after much deliberation; in reality I was pausing to catch my breath between each word.

We started digging into a bank of snow, steeper than the slope we had climbed, intending to burrow horizontally into the hillside in a narrow tunnel before making a larger cavern. The site was some incalculable distance below the crest of the West Shoulder. Pete thought it to be only a short distance; I thought it would take at least an hour to climb. I am not sure if it is an effect of altitude or simply lack of objects by which to estimate scale, but gauging distance is a difficult and often disappointing exercise on a mountain.

Ten minutes of digging was enough to tire us, so we took it in turns. The snow was perfect for excavation. Unlike the Eskimos, who have dozens of words for snow, our language is limited. If there was a word to describe the ideal snow for a snow cave, it would have applied to the snow we were digging, firm without being icy. I took a turn, kneeling in the deepening shaft we now had running into the hillside, the white snow of the surface turning blue in the inner recesses of the shaft with the diffusion of light through it. I noticed a black mark at the end of the tunnel which by this time was six feet deep. Suspecting a rock, which would render our efforts futile, I struck at it and the snow around gave way to reveal a dark hole. At first I recoiled in shock, but when nothing more happened I crawled forward and stared down into a gaping crevasse, totally enclosed with a roof of ice and festooned inside with fantastic formations of crystalline ice and blocks of snow, a winter wonder-land. Some huge blocks spanned the crevasse, forming a shelf; to the left the hole dropped away into bottomless blackness. I withdrew in awe and motioned Pete to look in.

Crevasses have connotations of terror for a mountaineer and my first instinct was to start afresh elsewhere. Pete was similarly nonplussed. If it was sensible to use the crevasse as a shelter it would save us two days of excavation, but if it was unstable we could wake up to a slow death from suffocation or a plunge into a newly opened chasm.

We decided to enter the crevasse and examine from inside its potential. We kept the rope fastened to our waists and tied to some stakes driven firmly into the snow outside, a lifeline to safety. I dropped inside onto the shelf, feeling as if I was entering forbidden territory, with the nervousness of a burglar on his first job. We took up separate stances and flailed away with ice axes at the ice formations hanging from the roof. The roof was only a couple of feet thick in parts and a blue, suffused light penetrating the snow illuminated the interior. We used the: snow knocked down from the ceiling to level the floor, and as we grew more at home in this, icy fairyland I crawled to the furthest end in one direction where the cave funnelled down to a cone, and the bright light showed that the roof was thinnest. I knocked down with a sense of regret the weird, fantastical formations, widening the cave. Pete worked on making a new entrance as the hole we had dropped in through was eight feet above the floor. After a couple of hours, completely at ease in this pit now, we had enlarged the cave sufficiently for three people to sleep inside, with plenty more space that could be easily cleared. We were well pleased with our work; in a matter of hours we had ready a cave which we had thought would take days to prepare, and in two days we had broken through the psychological barrier which had surrounded Camp 2.

When we came to leave we had difficulty escaping. Pete, tunnelling away to make a new entrance, had been doing so directly below the hole by which we had entered. There was fifteen feet of snow to dig through and he had only partially completed it. Thus, there was a gaping cavity and nothing on which to stand to reach the upper hole. I struggled and berated Pete before managing to claw my way out. Pete similarly struggled, much to my satisfaction.

We had let ourselves have an easier day now that we had achieved our objective. We reached the tent at Camp 2 comfortably before dark and transmitted the happy news of our fortunate discovery. Pete and I intended to ferry all our gear up from Camp 2 to the snow cave, Camp 3, next day, before going down for a rest.

The radio call brought bad news. Wan Chup, the cook, was critically ill and Pete was asked to consider going down in his capacity as doctor. He had the symptoms described to him over the radio, vomiting, delirium and excretion of blood. Pete guessed at a perforated ulcer. The doctor from the Italian camp had come over, but if there was no improvement Pete resigned himself to descending next morning.

It had always been a *bête noire* of Pete's, that just such a conflict would arise between his responsibility as a doctor and his wishes as a climber. There was no other option, Wan Chup did seem seriously ill, and although Pete was the first to acknowledge that doctors cannot wave magic wands, if Wan Chup died the whole expedition would be stigmatized for its irresponsibility if it was known that the doctor was out of reach on the mountain.

Pete's face wore a look of glumness for the rest of the evening. I agreed that his first responsibility was to descend, but I regretted to see him go. This had been the first time I had had anything to do with him on the expedition and I had come to realize that the anonymous person who kept in the background, who had not seemed to be going as strongly as some, was in fact driven by a. purposeful determination. Perhaps he had been overshadowed by the extrovert garrulousness of some of us or was simply pacing himself until he had found his own level. Whatever the explanation, I was now impressed at the new person I had seen emerge in the last couple of days. There was every reason for all of us to be mystified by Pete. He seemed genuinely to enjoy being on his own, often walking for hours at a time far from the company of anyone. Before we reached Base Camp he sometimes went off on a solo sortie, soaking up new sights without needing to share the experience. On the mountain we had grown accustomed to his eccentric tendency to set off late and often arrive so late that we came to call him the Midnight Cowboy.

I felt a fraud beside him. Suddenly on returning to the tent I was overcome with fatigue but, obliged by the pact of my own instigation on the cooking of meals; I had to prepare: the food. I spent the next three hours melting snow and making drinks and meals. These I passed to a reclining Pete who seemed unaffected by the exertions of the last two days and devoured everything I gave him. After heating the water for the main meal, I realized that I could not face eating it, so I handed a huge panful of lasagne to Pete. I had the useless satisfaction of seeing him for the first time unable to finish a meal.

Another squashed and restless night passed, worse than the last, listening to Pete's groans, to the wind outside and finally capitulating to the recurring temptation to take a sedative in the search for sleep.

Pete gave me a brew of tea before leaving in the morning. An earlier than usual radio call told him of the anxious vigil kept beside Wan Chup's feverish bed by the members down below. Reluctantly he left and I dropped off to sleep, now that I was no longer constricted. I woke at midday with a clear head and hurried to ready myself before Ade arrived and caught me still in bed.

It was 1 p.m. when he reached the tent on his way to the cave above. I had a warm drink ready for him but he still mocked my idleness. He continued on to the cave and I followed, glad at the thought that I would be spending no more nights in that tent. As I toiled, heavy laden, up the same slopes for the third day running, the snow turned pink with the setting sun. Far below, a red matchstick man appeared by the tent of Camp 2. It was Paul on his way up, but it would be dark before he reached the cave.

Paul had stopped off at Camp 2 and added even more weight to his monstrous, heavy load. His familiar hearty laugh had something of a chagrined resignation to it now. Ade gave out news of the air of discouragement which was hanging over Base Camp. It was the middle of January and the feeling was that the attempt to climb the West Ridge was turning into a war of attrition which was taking a heavy toll. There had been discussion about fixing a date in early February for the porters to arrive and for us to leave Base Camp if we were not in striking distance of the summit.

This was demoralizing news, especially so in contrast to the euphoria of the progress of the last few days. If only everyone could have a couple of perfect days on the mountain such as Pete and I had experienced, attitudes would change and morale would be restored.

The cave at Camp 3 was spacious, and consequently much colder than Camp 1. A constant draught streamed up, seemingly from the bowels of the mountain, through the black hole at the far end of the cave. Paul, for all his fatigue, could not eat much as he had developed an aversion to the freeze-dried food we had and which was the mainstay of our diet. It was an unpleasant night, the three of us, huddled together, unembarrassed, to share our bodily warmth.

At night we slept totally enclosed in our sleeping bags, still wearing every bit of clothing except boots. The hood of the sleeping bags could be drawn closed round the head, leaving, only a small hole for ventilation. We woke each morning to an icy layer surrounding the hole, formed as breath condensed and froze to the outer surface of the bag.

By luck the cave at Camp 3 was in the lee of the West Ridge, sometimes gaining protection from the wind. On the morning after our first night in the cave, Paul volunteered to spend the day improving the accommodation and digging the new entrance. Pete's excavations were still unfinished and entry to or exit from the cave still necessitated negotiating an eight-foot drop. Paul's task was to burrow through fifteen feet of snow outwards from the floor level of the cave and to block in the first entrance.

I felt that Ade and I had the more desirable option; we set off to reach the West Shoulder, to investigate the route along the crest of the ridge to Camp 4. Words do not emanate of themselves the slowness, of movement, the lassitude at such heights; memory cheats and passes over the blank spaces between events; half an hour to put on boots and then strap on crampons sounds ridiculous but is normal. Life on this mountain was a slow-motion actuality.

We were ready to leave, hovering on the outside of the cave; the momentary hesitation before breaking new ground, the slight reluctance too first. Ade pulled out his bar of chocolate-coated mint cake: 'Should give me energy,' he said. 'I need it.' It sounded a good idea, though I was not a follower of the Burgess devotion to diet control and energy foods. I ate a few squares and Ade swallowed all his. 'You've not eaten a whole bar, have you?' I was incredulous at his capacity to consume so much of the same sickly sweetmeat at one go. 'I need it to get up there,' he laughed, intrigued by my astonishment, and he strode off powerfully upwards as if to make his point.

The snow was firm and the crampons held securely. Crack lines crossed the surface and we came upon an area of larger crevasses. At any other season these would have been worrying illustrations of the lethal mobility of the slope, but one of the few advantages of winter was proving to be that movement of the snow, as well as of humans, was, if not stopped completely, considerably slowed down. We were reasonably sure that there was no danger of avalanche.

Sparkling streamers of snow came whirling over the West Shoulder as we neared the crest and climbed into the wind. Ade was a distance ahead and, unwilling to capitulate to his credence in diet-determining performance, I busied myself taking photographs of his silhouette against the rising sun, thus disguising, my slower pace.

We carried ropes and snow stakes, but were not using the ropes for the moment. Though icy, the angle of the slope was easy. A slip could mean a fatal, uncontrollable 5,000-feet slide but this was our medium; this was the everyday routine of a mountaineer as familiar or dangerous as driving a car. The growing wind, tugging at my body, heightened my concentration; in my hand was an ice axe, a third support, held ready to drive into the ice to arrest any fall. The silhouette above disappeared over the crest of the ridge. I could not hurry to catch up; I could only continue at the same steady pace, frequently halting, and enjoying the sight of Pumori, which towers above Base Camp, dropping away below.

Ade was sitting on a lone rock protruding from a rounded plateau of wind-hardened snow, bending now against the force of the wind. There was probably a smile on his face but ice masked his mouth and goggles concealed his eyes. Behind him a huge panorama unfolded – the walls of Everest. Lhotse and Nuptse formed an arc round the deep basin of the Western Cwm, one of the, forbidden places of the earth. The Cwm is the valley leading to these mountains, the entrance, to which is guarded by the formidable Khumbu Icefall. We were surrounded now by mountains, snowy ranks receding into the distance on every side. A few years ago I would have found the sight appalling, so many mountains to climb, so much suffering to reach their summits, so much effort needed and so many doubts about my own ability and resolve. Now I had come to know that I would not stop climbing; this mountain scene was exhilarating rather than oppressive, full of endless opportunity. Sometimes I feel as if mountains have become an addiction, the pleasure gone, the compulsion to partake remaining. Rarely blessed with the enjoyment of the moment, I had come to realize the satisfaction of going to the limit, physically and mentally, of dipping into danger and exhaustion, of returning full of enthusiasm for life and appreciation for every part of existence.

My feet trudged on over the humps of the plateau. Ade said he was feeling the altitude but I pressed him to go further. The plateau narrowed to a ridge, the ridge reared up, a knife-edge of snow running into the summit pyramid which now looked close. To our right the slope fell away steeply, 3,000 feet to the bottom of the Cwm. I was tired too. Only the desire to reach the Shoulder and see a new panorama, after weeks on the slopes below, had driven me up. Ever-cautious, Ade was, wary of going too far along the ridge. The wind was gusting strongly; if it gained more strength it could easily pick us up and throw us over the ridge or drop us into the Western Cwm. We agreed on a point to reach before turning back, but we had been looking at different points, and when the ridge steepened to an angle where it would have been foolish to continue without ropes, Ade suggested that we had come far enough for the day.

We had reached 24,000 feet. The remainder of the ridge looked more difficult but providing the wind was not too strong we should be able to reach a site for Camp 4. It would have to be another cave, gruelling as, its excavation might be, at 25,000 feet. Beyond, that a ramp of snow cut diagonally leftwards, into the North Face to a narrow gully slicing the vast yellow rock area of Everest's summit pyramid. That was the last major obstacle. We fastened our sacks of gear to a stake driven into the snow and turned back, well pleased.

We descended to Camp 3, pilgrims returning from some holy shrine. The distance we had covered was vast and descending required total concentration, but we were back with Paul before the afternoon was far gone.

The new entrance was ready, the old one sealed with blocks of snow, but light came through this thinner layer and through chinks between the blocks. The cave inside was illuminated as by the patterned windows of a clerestory.

Alan flopped into the cave unannounced at the end of the afternoon. We had not established satisfactory radio communication yet from Camp 3 so we were uncertain about the movements of anyone else on the mountain. Alan let us know that John was due to arrive at the Lho La that afternoon and should be on his way to Camp 3 the next day.

Paul had hardly eaten since he had arrived. A drink and some soup was all that he could manage. He was apologetic, seeing this inadequacy as detrimental to his own strength and therefore the strength of the team. It was a little more uncomfortable with four of us; there was plenty of room, we were utilizing perhaps only one-third of the cave, but only this third was widened and levelled for use. At the far end was the bottomless pit which we would never fill but which provided us with the luxury of an indoor toilet.

Alan had the worst position, at the edge of the levelled area, using rucksacks to increase his sleeping space. Paul and Ade in the middle were warmest, sheltered from the draught by warm bodies on every side.

I was ready to go down next day, in need of a rest and making way for replacements. Paul felt he should descend as well, being too weak from lack of food to be capable of going further. Ade was listless after three days' continuous movement upwards. He intended to rest for a day before going up again. Only Alan was keen to do something positive; if nothing else he would descend to the now redundant Camp 2 and ferry up the remaining gear.

Alan crawled out through the tunnel and came back with the disheartening news that it was blowing a gale outside and snowing. He disappeared again after a while and when he did not return we presumed him to have gone to Camp 2. Paul made ready to go down, voicing his misgivings and expressing his anxiety that he might be obliged to return to Britain if the expedition was to go on much longer. He had given an optimistic forecast of his return as being the middle of January. It was now 18 January and if we went on it would be the middle of February before we got back. Paul was a college lecturer and had a more rigid timetable than most of us.

Rather than leave Ade without the certainty of a partner, I decided to stay on another night. We passed the day eating and drinking as often as the motivation allowed. Night came without the return of Alan or the arrival of John. Spindrift had been blowing into the cave and we sealed off the entrance with rucksacks.

Although we could receive some radio transmissions, we were not in line of sight with Base Camp and our messages were not getting through. It takes a stronger signal to transmit than to receive and after several tries Ade gave up, though even from inside the cave we could sometimes hear the calls from Base. Al's flat voice came weakly over the air: 'Base to Lho La and Camp 2 or 3 do you read me?' repeated over and over. 'In case you are listening ... ' the words trailed on lost in the crackle of interference.

'Just listen to our kid's voice,' complained Ade in disgust. 'If he put some expression into it we might be able to pick something up. He's just droning away.'

There was an uneasy feeling about the way things were going. I was not much use at the moment. I had been on the mountain for ten days and knew I needed a rest if I was going to contribute anything more. The question was growing whether Everest really was too difficult in winter. Certainly the cold was more insupportable, sleep was difficult and headaches were more frequent than usual. Even inside a down suit and a sleeping bag feet were nearly always chilled. On eating a meal, warmth could be felt percolating down: to the toes as combustion of, the food took place. As a topic of conversation this often replaced the weather in its popularity.

The Burgesses have the disadvantage of being unable to sleep on their sides. Alan put forward the explanation as being the width of their shoulders, no pillows being high enough to support their heads. Whatever the reason, Ade was forced to lie on his back, facing upwards to a ceiling, a couple of feet above him, which was festooned with 'long, gangly, white fronds', as he described them. Each time he coughed, a shower of these fronds descended, dislodged by the slightest movement of air. The cave was anyway filled with the fine particles of snow driven in by the wind through any crevice. A torch beam would lance through the air, catching the floating particles in its light like a beam from the lamp of a bus in a London fog. In one wall of the cave was an unsuspected crack to the outside through which fine snow was pouring. It was the worst night yet in a cave.

Powder snow covered everything when we woke. A dim light filtered into the cave; there was no sound of the wind. There was no increase in warmth with the morning, the thermometer showing a steady -20 degrees Celsius. I put some lumps of snow into a pan and lay back waiting for it to melt.

Two hours later I prepared to go down to Camp 2 to clear it of any remaining gear. Ade needed to rest further. I pulled aside the rucksacks blocking the exit. A small shaft remained of our tunnel; the rest was filled for fifteen feet with snow. At the far end of the shaft sunlight caught the snow. The storm was over but we were snowed in.

When I dug the tunnel clear and popped through, to the outside it was still blustery, but there were clearings in the sky, and the force of the storm was spent. A new, crisp, whiteness coated the mountainside and the ropes leading down were buried.

I ferried up more sleeping bags and food from Camp 2, and brought the ruined tent to use as a curtain on our tunnel. Gradually we were improving our living quarters.

No one else arrived that day and with little remaining reserves of strength after eleven days on the mountain I resolved to descend next day. Ade too was tired and he came down. Deep banks of snow covered the slopes, and our steps dislodged these, precipitating small avalanches. It was better that we should, do this than wait for a dangerous accumulation to form and an overwhelming avalanche to sweep down of its own volition. The wind was constant but not too strong. I was stumbling, but it was from fatigue rather than the wind.

Near the bottom a lone figure was coming upwards. It was John, distinguishable by the colour of his clothes. He was covered in snow from pulling clear the ropes and caked blood from some unmentioned mishap was mingled with the ice on his face when we met him. With the lack of radio communication we had come to an awkward imbalance of movement on the mountain. John, on his own, would be able to achieve little at Camp 3 and I did not envy him his lone vigil up there till someone from below should join him.

John had been at Camp 1 on the night of the most recent storm and he had a woeful tale of waking to find that he too was snowed in. Desperate to relieve himself, he had done so into a plastic bag and disposed of it hours later when he had finally dug himself free.

Troubled with doubts about the present situation on the mountain, we left John moving upwards and ourselves trailed on to Base Camp.

Enthusiasm at the progress we had to report was tempered by the general gloom about our chances of success. There had been more sickness in the camp.

At our instigation Brian, Pete and Al went up, in spite of ominous weather signs, to the Lho La and we entered a period of discussion at Base Camp about tactics and our prospects.

By afternoon it was snowing steadily. We were anticipating the arrival of the mail runner but had doubts about the likelihood of his bringing any mail. Two Sherpas, however, arrived first, one of them, Nima Norbu, being our new Sirdar to replace Dawa. He brought unwelcome news of knee-deep snow down at Syangboche and the unlikelihood of flights into the airstrip for many days.

Base Camp was no longer a comfortable place. Since before Christmas we had had few spells of fine weather. The tents sagged under the weight of snow, and even if a day started clear, clouds usually enveloped the sky before it was out and the camp was little more than a bleak, chill wasteland. I began to prefer the idea of being back on the mountain – at least there I expected to be uncomfortable, to have to struggle to survive. I felt cheated here and annoyed when I found that at every moment of the day I was conscious of being cold.

A scrapyard of blackened, useless stoves lay outside the cook tent. One by one our stoves, paraffin and petrol alike, had packed up under the extremes of winter, fourteen stoves in all. Alan and Brian had gone on, a borrowing mission to the Japanese camp and returned with two enormous paraffin stoves which we hoped would last us for the rest of the expedition.

The Japanese equally were stalled by the conditions on the mountain. As well as being shaken by the death of one of their members, several others of the climbers and five Sherpas were frostbitten. Some of the Japanese displayed on their cheeks and noses the tell-tale purple weals of once-frozen flesh; one of the Sherpas was going to need part of his foot amputating and another some fingers. A train of yaks had been summoned, to carry them down to the airstrip, and hospital.

On 20 January three Japanese had left their Base Camp to go back up for one final attempt. The Italians, attempting Lhotse, had not made much progress beyond the trail which they shared with the Japanese to the foot of their mountain. From the start they had seemed lost in face of their objective, with clothing and tentage hardly different from what they would use in the Alps. They too, were running out of steam.

The only way to obtain a semblance of warmth was to sit in a tent, when the sun was out, with the doors zipped closed to exclude the breeze. The heat of the sun on the tent walls raised the temperature inside to a luxurious degree and, though the sociable atmosphere of the dining tent was better than solitude, the rare opportunity of restoring circulation was too good to miss.

I lay there one day enjoying the solar heating and the glowing feel of warmth returning to my feet, thinking over events. At 7 a.m. I had listened in to Ade making the radio call to the Lho La. The sky had been unsettled but held the promise of clearing. His brother was exhausted after breaking trail for several hours up to the Lho La. The walls and slabs of rock were much changed from when we had first climbed them. Snow a foot deep concealed footholds arid left the hands numb from groping through it to find purchase. The journey to Camp 1 took twice as long. Brian had had a bad night and did not feel like moving Ade exhorted his brother to persuade Pete to go on up to Camp 3 where John from whom we had heard nothing since passing him on the way up, was still alone.

By 9 a.m. the sky was really overcast and on a second, prearranged radio call, Ade was told that the weather on the Lho La was atrocious but Pete had left nevertheless to relieve the beleaguered John. It was good news – at least there was some activity.

From the experience of reaching the West Shoulder I was convinced that given good weather we could climb this mountain. The Shoulder is at a height of approximately 24,000 feet and it had felt similarly bad to 24,000 feet on any other mountain at other times of the year. The main difference was the force of the wind, the deadly cold and the rapidity with which the weather could change. 'If only the weather would hold,' I wrote in my diary. 'I won't mind the suffering involved; I do not think that the cold plus lack of oxygen plus dry air will be what will stop us.'

This sort of expedition was not something to become addicted to and subconsciously the conviction had formed that if we should get up Everest this time I would not come again to the Himalayas in winter. I wrote further: 'I suppose I have always connected mountaineering at its limit with arduous, almost unbelievable hardship, for our generation this is it – the Himalayas in winter, when a few short hours of warmth are all one can expect, if lucky'.

A commotion outside heralded the arrival of Mingma, our cook boy, who was now acting as mail runner. In spite of the lack, of flights he had some mail to offer; residue from a previous flight or brought by some other mysterious route we could not fathom. Disappointingly, there was no newspaper. We were all together in the dining tent, Graham rocking back and forth on his feet trying to encourage the circulation, the brief sun of midday now concealed behind grey clouds.

Ade and I had been insistent, on coming back to Base Camp from Camp 3, that there should be people on the mountain at each of the camps all the time, and that if the weather was bad they should stick it out ready to push the route further or move up to relieve those at the front. These ideas came out of our own experience of waiting for support and seeing John going up on his own with no back-up. But the continuing hostile weather, and now the news that Pete was forcing his way up to Camp 3 in a storm, was taken as a rebuttal of this suggestion.

Alan advocated waiting until the weather did clear and then having everyone move on the mountain together in the hope of doing eight man-days of work instead of two with the rotation system.

We had reached 23 January. Our permission for Everest was due to expire on the 31st of the month. Alan had used the Japanese radio connection with Kathmandu to ask for an extension of our permit. We were granted an extra two weeks.

Food and fuel were running short and our diet had become very monotonous. The question of arranging a date for departure arose once again. Still enthusing from the positive progress I had been involved in, I argued against any suggestion of fixing a date for departure 'If we state that we will leave by a certain date, we will have already decided on the outcome of the expedition.

Psychologically we will have given up. We should not be thinking of how efficiently we can leave, but of continuing, if there is a chance of getting up the mountain, even after our permit has run out.

Alan pointed out that such an action would inevitably alienate the government of Nepal, since in the past they had reacted strongly against anyone breaking their rules.

'Climbing is all about breaking rules. It's in the nature of the game. Would the North Face of the Eiger ever have been climbed if the climbers of the day had abided by the laws laid down forbidding any attempt on it? We should think of extending the permission again, sending down for more food and fuel, not letting their lack, dictate our movements.'

As official leader, Alan was in an invidious position. Any one of the rest of us could do as he wished, break any number of laws, but the responsibility lay with the leader and the sanction most often enforced is to ban the leader from Nepal for a number of years. For a keen climber this was anathema, especially if the punishment was enforced for an action of someone other than himself.

Basically there was agreement that at some stage we would have to make a decision about leaving; we could not stay forever. Alan and Brian, as the two who shouldered most of the burden of organization, wanted to have considered the practicalities and time-scales involved in departing from the mountain. It was agreed that a certain amount of good weather was necessary for success and that by the end of the month we would have a clear idea of the likely outcome. Allen Jewhurst volunteered to stay behind as long as need be in Kathmandu to clear up any formalities and forward the gear if this would set minds at rest regarding delays in getting home.

The discussion cleared the air. There was a renewed sense of commitment to stick it out to the end. Photographs, maps and books, were pored over and passed round to glean every bit of information and encouragement. The contours of the: summit pyramid were compared on the map with those of other known areas of the mountain and the final chapters of the book by Hornbein and Unsoeld on their ascent of Everest, triumphing at the eleventh hour against all the odds, were taken as an example.

Conversation drifted down from the intense level of the afternoon and by evening, after an unsuccessful radio call at 6 p.m., we were given to musing on more light-hearted subjects. The abominable snowman entered the conversation and its existence on Everest, as reported by the Japanese, given as a reason for the lack of communication from those at Camp 1 on the Lho La.

Alan developed on this theme and went off into a wild fantasy about Pete and his ferocious appetite, sketching out a scenario of the climbers who vanish one by one, from the Lho La with only Pete surviving, growing fatter and fatter, to be last seen making off down the Rongbuk glacier. Ade summed up the erosion of our senses after so long in the mountains as he tried to make out a list of basic equipment needed for his next expedition. When, after an hour of pondering, he had only three items on his list, he looked up with a puzzled expression and said:

'It's hard to think, after a few weeks here, isn't it?'

10   Attrition and the Turning Point

January 24 dawned snowy and dull. Depression seemed to hang above and below. However, radio communications were at last effective. Pete had taken up with him some wire with which he had rigged up an extension aerial and the same had been done at the Lho La. Communications could now be conducted froth the comfort of the sleeping bags inside the caves.

There was no progress above Camp 3. John had been hit by a return of amoebic dysentery and was trying to nurture his strength to descend. Brian and Al lower down at Camp 1 had attempted to go on up to Camp 3 but had had to retreat after being battered and tossed about by the winds.

Paul and Alan were ready to go up onto the mountain but whilst no progress was possible for anyone up there they stayed at Base Camp where the energy drain was less. Paul had misgivings about voicing the need for his return home, not wanting to undermine the momentum of the trip. He stated briefly and clearly why he would have to leave, intending by so doing to put his case and then let it be forgotten. He was going up one more time, knowing that there was no possibility of his reaching the summit in the time left, but meaning to help the expedition for as long as he could.

Maurizio, the lone Italian at their Base Camp, frequently visited us in his search for company. He was not a climber but had come with the expedition to act as interpreter. The rest of his friends were at Camp 2 in the Western Cwm, his only contact with them for many days being by radio. True to style, the Italian cuisine was, enlivened with blocks of parmesan cheese, hunks of ham and other long-forgotten delicacies. By one means or another Brian, a ruthless negotiator, had managed to strike an extraordinary bargain by which we obtained a selection of these in exchange for some of the freeze-dried food for the mountain, of which we had an abundance and for which most of us by now had acquired a hearty aversion. For a time the much loathed 'noodle stew', to which we had been reduced, was kept at bay.

The Japanese encampment had an air of gloom too. We were always welcome and for a change of scene one or two people would pay them a visit from time to time. The visits had grown more frequent in an endeavour to obtain a more accurate assessment of the weather: They had their 'facsimile' machine which reproduced a weather map transmitted from Delhi. And received a weather report by radio from Kathmandu from a team member who had returned there to sort out formalities after the death of one of their group.

The map and reports bore little relation to the mountains by which we were surrounded. Such convoluted terrain creates its own weather and all we could look for from the broadcast information was a general trend. On 24 January the Japanese informed us that the information they had received was that it was impossible to make any predictions for the next week. The weather map was a mass of tightly packed lines covering the whole Indian sub-continent.

The members of their own team were stuck at Camp 2. They had tried to make progress to Camp 3 and up to the South Col but had been forced back by wind and poor visibility. Now their food was running very low. They could not descend to Base Camp because the route through the icefall had been destroyed with the collapse of several walls of ice, ruining the bridges across crevasses which they had so laboriously built. A repair party from below would have to go up first to replace the ladders.

There was a set of bathroom scales at the Japanese camp and we weighed ourselves. Alan and Graham had lost two stones. They were both gaunt, lean figures compared to their normal appearance. All of us believed we had lost weight but found there was little or no variation from our normal weights. Ade found he had put on weight, a discovery which made him feel much better.

A hurricane roared all night over the Lho La. I lay in the comfort and security of my Base Camp tent listening uneasily, aware of the demoralizing effect the wind would have on Al and Brian in the cave of Camp 1. The 'mortar bomb simulation' would be pounding all night. Later in the day an apologetic Al and Brian arrived back, justifying their departure from Camp 1 by describing the debilitating effect, physically and mentally, of lying for day after day in the ice cave, waiting for the weather to improve. They felt themselves losing strength all the while and had decided to come down.

The wind did not touch us at Base Camp but just after sunset a roar which was not the wind had brought us rushing from the dining tent to see, vague and formless in the twilight, a billowing cloud of avalanche debris pouring out of the 'Burgess couloir'. One of the ice cliffs at the edge of the Lho La, had collapsed. A grey, seething wall of snow advanced imperceptibly, menacingly towards the camp. Outlying streamers flung a dusting of powder snow over us and our tents, but the main mass passed by, its force largely spent in its journey of over a mile. Ade had a wry grin on his face when we had settled back into the tent.

After dark a very wasted and weary-looking John pushed his way into the dining tent. He spoke of the horror of life at Camp 3 during the storms, of the cold and the snow which forced itself in through every tiny crevice and the subsequent maelstrom of whirling snow inside. He had become very weak from dysentery and had had no option but to descend, sorry himself not to have gone further and leaving behind a disappointed Pete who was equally unable to make any progress on his own. John's experience at Camp 3 had been quite an ordeal, culminating, as he describes it himself, in a disturbed night and harrowing descent:

> The night in the cave was one long groan. The cold penetrated deep into my bones. Sleep was impossible. The moment I dozed off, my breathing became fitful and irregular. I would open my eyes, gasping for air in the frozen, roaring blackness. At first I felt unutterably fatigued.
>
> By 11 a.m. I knew I had to descend. Diarrhoea had returned, and through coughing so much I had developed a severe pain in my chest. I was worried that pneumonia might set in.
>
> Outside, the weather was bad but no worse than on the days I had hauled loads up from Camp 2. Pete, keen to go on, was disappointed at my decision to go down, but he knew I had no choice. I fell over frequently as I tried to make ready to descend.
>
> Getting down the ropes was a nightmare. The wind blew me over unexpectedly from one direction and then the other. I was attached to the rope at all times, but once I heard an unmistakable 'click', just as I was about to launch off down the rock barrier, as the karabiner which fastened my harness to the rope came unclipped. Without emotion I re-secured it and continued.
>
> I was only halfway down when my diarrhoea overcame me, adding to my suffering. I could not stop. When I reached the Lho La the wind was too strong for me to walk. I crawled the half mile back to the caves, still being blown over by the wind and bouncing along like a ball. My cherished hope was that someone would be waiting for me at Camp 1 with a mug of tea ready, but the caves were empty. I dug the snow from the entrance before crawling in and beginning the ignominious task of cleaning myself up.
>
> I still felt extremely ill and decided to continue the descent, lest I should be unable to do so next day if I stayed.
>
> Only when I reached the rocks at the start of the descent did I become aware of the time. I had no strength to hurry, but forced myself down in a slow, dazed routine, checking and rechecking before I made a move. I reached the glacier at dusk.
>
> 'Not long now,' I reassured myself, relaxing slightly as I switched on my head torch. But where I had expected to find a familiar trail there was only soft, deep snow and avalanche debris. Soon it was completely dark and the light from my

torch began to fail. Unfamiliar ice towers appeared all round and I sank through the soft snow at every second step, expecting each time to find the blackness of a crevasse rushing up towards me. I was lost, and the only solution was to retrace my steps and find somewhere to spend the night out.

Adrenalin kept me going and I had almost regained the edge of the glacier when I caught sight in the distance of the light of someone moving about at Base Camp. Relief penetrated my exhaustion and I trudged in the direction of the light. New, snow obscured all tracks, but I knew the way now. I wondered if I would recover strength to go up again. There was the noise of chatter from the dining tent, I entered and the bright light and warmth hit me like the memory of a lost world.

John could stomach no food and retired to his tent early. It was sickening to wake to a fine day on 26 January. This was the first fine day for some time and there would be no progress still. Alan and Paul left to re-occupy Camp 1.

Late in the afternoon we caught sight of Paul through the telephoto lens nearing the top of the steep corner. He and Alan had been delayed by the deep snow which still covered the route and when there was no reply to the radio call at 6pm it was an indication that they would probably be too tired next day to go on up to Camp 3. Towards evening the clouds blew up swiftly from the south.

The plan was for Ade and myself to go up the next day, hoping, to occupy Camp 1 as Paul and Alan went on up to Camp 3, and for us to wait there until we could move up to replace them after they had pushed the route further and retired for a rest. Pete was also up at Camp 3, but he would be in need of a rest after being stranded there for several days through some bad storms. The basic business of survival in such cold and at such altitudes is a trying ordeal.

John was the other person who had a formal job to return to by a certain date. However, he dismissed such anxieties as he felt and resigned himself to the prospect of finding he had no job left on his return. He wanted to stay till the end.

As Ade and I left next morning to go back onto the mountain I called by John's tent to see how he was.

'Much better thanks Joe, I should be able to get back up there the day after tomorrow.'

Relieved at John's recovery, Ade and I set off, Ade at his usual steady rhythm with me panting behind. He even tempted me up the quicker route of the 'Burgess Couloir', reasoning that any loose stuff would, have been dislodged by the cataclysmic avalanche of two days ago.

As we reached the steep walls of the corner, Pete came into view, sliding swiftly down the ropes. Pete always seemed to be carrying a sack with something in it. Most of us tried to conserve energy and in descent carry nothing at all. For whatever reason, possibly to make sure that he always had extra clothing to hand, Pete's sack usually looked full.

He was reluctant to be going down, he said, but he had broken a rib. There had been no accident but he had never shaken off the hacking cough by which he had been troubled for weeks now. During a prolonged bout of coughing one of his ribs had cracked.

'Does that mean you are out of it now for the rest of the trip?'

'Oh no, it's happened before and it got better. In another few days I should be okay!'

It was news to me that he had broken a rib earlier but now I realized the reason for his groans at night when he had shared the tent at Camp 2 and marvelled at his taciturnity.

'See you soon then,' and I continued to Camp 1.

When we arrived at the cave, Alan was in residence. Paul had left early in the day for Camp 3 and could be seen as a tiny speck of red on the way up to the West Shoulder. The cave was as familiar as home. Supplies were a little more sparse and the ceiling above the cooking area was blackened with the soot from an accident with a stove. Otherwise nothing had changed.

Alan busied himself melting snow and passing us drinks. He was still racked with frequent coughs and periodically, as if by auto-suggestion, I found that I too was succumbing to a bout. Once started, there was no escape. The cold, dry air compounded the irritation in the throat and the victim's body would be shaken by the hacking cough until randomly flung free of its spell. The nights at Base as well as on the mountain were often broken by staccato bursts of noise disturbing the sleep of the sufferer and all those around.

On the radio we heard that the Japanese had called a halt to their expedition and had started evacuating the mountain. In the little time that they had left they had no hope of the weather improving sufficiently to enable them to reach the summit. The Italians too were doubtful of their chances and with the Japanese withdrawing, the way up the ice-fall would be more difficult to maintain. Inevitably these items of news turned us to discussion of our own situation. If we did not, make some very definite progress on this attempt, we too would have little hope of climbing the mountain. Alan reckoned that we needed ten days of good weather if we were to stand a chance.

One improvement at Camp 1 had been the construction by Pete of a toilet. Previously we had used the bare hillside, digging a small hole as the need arose. Since the Lho La was rarely free from wind, 'going to the toilet' at any time, but especially at night, was a most undesirable ordeal. Our clothing was designed to allow the performance of the necessary functions by means of long zips that removed the need to undress completely. Nevertheless, a substantial area of the back and buttocks was still exposed. The operation was usually completed with the greatest of haste and one scuttled back to the sheltering cave feeling decidedly vulnerable and helpless against the demands of nature which could come at any time of day or night. I had got into the habit on expeditions of trying to establish a discipline in my bodily rhythms of only going to the toilet once a day, and that once in the morning. That way the whole business was completed along with all the other morning duties, otherwise it might mean disentangling oneself from harnesses and ropes and performing in even more precarious and unpleasant situations.

Even at the Lho La camp the problem was that whichever way one faced, the wind would always find the weak spot and even reaching a suitable place was a tricky manoeuvre with the risk of slipping or being blown down the slope outside the cave. We wore all of our clothes all the time, except boots, and the sensible thing to do was to dress completely in crampons, mitts and ice axe, but this conflicted with the tendency to want to rush outside, get the job over with quickly, and get back inside a warm sleeping bag once more.

So Pete, in a labour of love, had worked on his own for some hours digging a trench into the hillside and erecting a wall with blocks of snow on three sides of the trench. It was crude but effective and although the narrow track to the toilet became icy with use, most of the danger was taken out of this necessary function and Pete had the satisfaction of having built a toilet with the most splendid view in the world down into Tibet, overlooked by the summit of Everest and flanked by the walls of Nuptse.

Long after dark, lingering over the evening meal which was enlivened by some bacon from the exchange with the Italians, there was an unfamiliar rustling outside and. Paul startled us when he burst in out of the night. He looked haggard and morose. He had climbed two-thirds of the way up to Camp 3 before coming to a standstill. For him the expedition had gone on too long, he had no reserves of energy, and pains in his back due to an attack of hepatitis a few months earlier had grown unbearable. It was almost night when he had turned back and he had realized by the slow progress he had made that he would be able to achieve little from Camp 3 anyway.

In the morning Paul was still in pain and he regretfully explained his decision to continue on down to Base Camp. For him the expedition was over. He expected to be gone before we got down again and we made our goodbyes.

'Give everyone a ring when you get back home, tell them we won't be long, will you?'

Without Paul we were missing a solid, reliable workhorse. Throughout he had been willing to fit in and perform some of the least exciting but essential roles. I was sorry to see him go.

Alan left first, crossing the Lho La towards the ropes. Ade and I tested each other's sacks, gauging the weight of food and gear we were taking up to Camp 3. Thirty-five to forty pounds, they didn't feel heavy outside the cave but half way to the bottom of the ropes they felt burdensome. We caught Alan up at the bergschrund where he was waiting to take some photographs. I loitered long enough to let Ade go in front – he seemed to have more energy than me – then I swung up the ropes after him and started the long, tedious haul to Camp 3, counting off each 150-foot-length of rope as I passed the anchor point: one gone, thirty five more ropes to go. Alan followed, always keeping at least one full rope length behind so that the weight of both of us was never on one anchor.

Ade soon outdistanced me, though Alan was going at the same pace. The three of us journeyed up hour after hour, separated by only a few hundred feet, without a word. The wind was strong enough to make us keep our hoods up, though the sky was clear. When I came through the trying stretches of the rock barrier, Ade was nowhere in sight. He had disappeared behind a rib of rock and from the top of it I could see jets of steam outlined by the sun which had not reached me yet revealing his location.

I never caught him up. Try as I might, my pace seemed slow, my sack a dead weight. When I reached the abandoned Camp 2, there were ten more rope lengths to go – almost there, only another hour and a half. Below, Alan had dropped back; he would be late.

The shadows were long down the Rongbuk glacier and the sun was setting before I arrived at Camp 3. I plunged inside down the long curving tunnel and grabbed the movie camera, an ancient Bolex. Outside, I filmed the boiling mass of clouds, spewing from the summit and catching the orange tints of the sinking sun. I was, awkward from the cold. The metal clung to my fingers as I risked using the camera without gloves and the warmth was sucked out of them by the cold casing. I made a clumsy mess of changing the film and tumbled back into the cave unsatisfied with my efforts but helpless from the pain of the cold in my hands.

It had taken me seven hours to reach Camp 3. Ade had done it in only five. Long after dark there was still no sign of Alan. The position of the cave precluded any sighting and only a descent of several hundred feet or a traverse across some precarious ice slopes would allow a view down to where he was last seen.

At 6 p.m., on the radio, Alan's voice came through from Camp 1. He too had ground to a halt well below Camp 3 and fearing benightment had descended while he still had strength and daylight left. We were relieved that he was safe but alarmed at the progressive weakening of the forces on the mountain. Alone again in this inhospitable ice chamber, Ade and I manoeuvred and shuffled like dogs in a new bed until we were ensconced in sleeping bags, food and stoves to hand and a pile of ice chunks ready for melting.

The hours of darkness in the Himalayas are long. In winter they were even more so, but sleep was harder to find. I was wary of taking any sleeping pills after the bad experiences the last time I was up. Consequently I passed a fitful night, my sleep disturbed for unknown reasons. Perhaps it was the cold draught through the cave, a particle of ice falling from the ceiling onto my face or contact with the ice-coated exterior of my sleeping bag as I turned over. Sometimes I was aware by his movements and altered breathing that Ade was awake too. I pestered him for the time. I had a watch, but to illuminate the face I had to press a button on the side. My fingers were too numb from the cold to do this.

Dawn's flat light filtered in through the walls of snow. The insulating mats on which we were sleeping were covered in, a fine layer of snow which had settled from the air in the night. Ade made moves to light the small gas stove and start the day.

I confessed to him that I felt nauseous and headachey. The prospect of doing anything was not appealing but to decide to make no move upwards today would mean further demoralization.

I got up to relieve myself and look outside. Beyond the crude curtain we now had over the entrance, the tunnel was lined with several inches of fresh snow. I crawled up it and poked my head out into a gale. Cloud was low and more snow was falling. I felt a guilty relief at the thought that we could justifiably have a day of rest. It would be too dangerous to go up onto the West Shoulder. At 8 a.m. we radioed down the situation. It was similarly wild at the Lho La, but Al and Brian were setting off from Base Camp to reach Camp 1.

Ade ministered to me all day making drinks and food. I was apologetic about my disability: 'I'm sorry I'm leaving you to do all the work.'

'That's okay, you did it for me last time.'

It was -21 degrees Celsius inside the cave; the only advantage it had over the cave lower down was that here we had an inside toilet.

In civilization one can hardly imagine passing a whole day and night lying next to a person with whom one is not emotionally involved. Little conversation passed between us, what little was to be said had already been reiterated many times in the weeks past. Making another cup of tea was an event as important as a dinner party, and took about as long to prepare. Gradually, through the administration of several pain killers and the intake of much liquid, my headache disappeared.

Even from Base Camp it was possible to misjudge the mountain. I sometimes used to wonder what could possibly stop us from putting one foot in front of the other, in making at least some progress. Lying in the cave was full of frustrations; we were drawn to satisfy our curiosity about the rest of the route, keen to advance a stage further. We could have gone outside, could have gone so far but without even discussing it we both knew the futility of such a gesture. A gesture as much demanded from within ourselves to ensure that we were not taking the soft option as from anything else.

I had spent a lot of time now with Ade and enjoyed the generous comradeliness of his company. He and his brother were quite different, I could see more clearly now, but different in a close way as if aspects of the same personality. This closeness seemed so strong that I was subconsciously surprised that they could perform independently of each other and made no obvious effort to make sure that they were teamed up. Ade was the more 'serious' of the two, often looking askance at the antics of his brother, who had a reputation for inadvertently wrecking things. Somehow a trenching tool had broken in his hands when digging a tent site at Camp 2; somehow the aerial on the master set of the radios had snapped when he was using it; somehow the syringe Pete had asked him to open in the tense moments round Wan Chup's sick bed had disintegrated in his hands. Al surfaced from each escapade with a self-mocking grin. One got the impression that Ade sometimes wanted to disown him.

Our food was a little better than it had been due to the discovery amongst the foods we had exchanged with the Italians of some easily cooked meals which tasted almost real. Tea and coffee had come to taste very acidic and the drink of preference was now one made from mineral salts and designed to help athletes. Whatever its benefits in that respect it made a refreshing change from tea and helped us consume the essential quantities of liquid.

The second night was as bad as the first. This time we both took a sleeping pill which Ade produced from his own little select pack of medicines. He assured me that they did not leave a nasty hangover like the others. We had too long to sleep though, and the effect of the pills wore off in the middle of the night leaving us back playing the waiting game to see if we could move at dawn.

Both of us felt queasy by morning. We were unsure why. There was plenty of air in the cave and we had both been to such altitudes many times before. It is not unusual to have headaches the first time one reaches a certain height during an expedition, but after several weeks one can expect to be completely acclimatized. We could only assume that it was caused by constantly breathing extremely cold air and having a cold draught passing over our faces.

Ade made the breakfast but I was on my knees retching for a while before I felt well enough to take anything. The day was clear but still windy. If we were to make any progress at all on the mountain we would have to resign ourselves to climbing, if it was possible, in the wind. We radioed down our intention of taking softie gear up onto the West Shoulder to assess conditions.

We took some coils of rope and digging tools each, intending to make a dump of gear along the ridge, thus easing the next day's work when we expected to go right through to the site for Camp 4. Since our loads were not too heavy we took a movie camera each, Ade the big, heavy Bolex and I the, smaller, cartridge loading Autoload. Mike was not to come any higher than the Lho La and now, in the absence of the professional, we felt less inhibited about our untutored efforts and also more responsibility to take film.

The Autoload was easy to handle. There were few controls and the cartridges were readily slotted in, even with mittened hands. A cartridge only lasted for sixty seconds though, hardly enough time to get into the rhythm of filming. Ade was off in front again and I tried to capture the ecstatic view of him silhouetted against the sun with streamers of wind-driven snow snaking down over the glistening ice and past his feet. There was no way of checking our results until we arrived back in Britain – it was a matter of shoot it and see.

Sixty seconds seemed a long time at altitude until I checked the film counter. The film had snapped with the cold. Without much regret, having tried to do my duty, I put the camera away. Anyway, as I reached the rounded plateau and I was occupied more and more with trying to keep my balance against the fierce gusts.

Ade was sitting on the same lone piece of black rock we had come across on our first visit here. He had the weighty Bolex pressed to his eye recording my erratic gait. For hand-held filming it is best not to breathe while the finger is actually on the trigger to avoid camera shake. Any effort to hold one's breath at altitude for more than a few seconds brought on a rapid, panicky gulping for air. The oxygen was already scarce enough without cutting it off completely. As I reached him, Ade pulled the camera away from his face. A white streak of frost-burn lined his nose where the cold metal of the camera case had frozen into place. Ade did not know it had happened till I shouted above the noise of the wind to take care. His whole face was numb and he would not feel any pain from the frost-burn until it warmed up. More of a perfectionist than me, he had taken his goggles off to see more, clearly through the viewfinder.

We soaked in the splendid panorama. Communication was hardly possible. The wind was far stronger than the first time we had come up to this point and to go further would be risky. This was a risk we felt we would have to take if we were going to get any further. Roped together would be the only way to advance, giving ourselves a chance of safeguarding each other against any slip. Sometimes I looked at the rest of the route as if it were just a short step, sometimes it seemed infinite. The only way to treat it was a little bit at a time.

We turned, to go back, dumping the gear beside the, rock, the incongruous spade, proof even against Al's latent destructiveness, was thrust into the snow to mark the spot. We believed we could make headway against the wind and would return next day, with luck with reinforcements, and make our way right along the ridge.

Back at Camp 3 we were puzzled to find no sign of any new arrivals. By dark still no one had arrived and the clear skies had gone, replaced by turbulent, snow-filled clouds.

We expected an explanation on the radio call but nothing came through from Camp I. From Base Camp we heard the alarming news that John had not recovered from his sickness and had left for home with Paul. Pete was on the radio and he explained that he had found John to have a chest infection as well as dysentery. John was unable to eat and had decided to leave for lower altitudes rather than grow progressively weaker trying to fight the illness in Base Camp.

A quarter of the strength of the team had thus vanished. Logically there were many reasons for Paul and John to have left but it was a savage blow and seemed to: mock our attempts at getting any further. There was no blame to attach to their decision to leave, Pete himself had been adamant on the radio that. John stood no chance of recovering, but with the arrogance of the fit I did feel a wordless frustration and fought hard within myself to maintain optimism. Their departure, however, compounded by the failure of anyone to arrive, aroused grave disquiet in our minds. For a couple of hours after dark Ade and I chewed over what was going on and whether up at Camp 3 we were as isolated and out on a limb as we felt. If no one was able to reach Camp 3, what prospect did we stand on our own? Certainly we could probably reach the site for Camp 4 and start digging a cave, but apart from the strain of working unsupported at such an altitude for several days we would soon run out of food and have to descend.

We resolved to do some straight talking next morning on the radio. If no one was coming up, would the risk involved in going further along the West Ridge worth taking? This night too passed with fitful sleep but this time it was for other reasons than the unpleasant physical conditions by which we were surrounded.

11 Straight Talking

Al came on the radio for the morning call. Ade spoke to him. It was the best possible pairing for a dialogue. Intimate as they were, with no means of subterfuge, these two could be more blunt and more open than most people ever could be to their closest friends.

Ade made the first call: 'Camp 3 to Lho La, come in please.'

Al replied 'Lola,' as he used to pronounce it, 'to Camp 3, hearing you loud and clear. How do you hear me? Over.'

'Loud and clear. What is going on? Why has no one come up? Do people intend to come up? Over.'

'It was too windy yesterday and no one here feeling is good. It is too windy again today to cross Lola.'

'Look, we went up to the West Shoulder yesterday to see what it was like. It was windy but we should be able to get further. If we can go up there in the wind you should be able to get up here.'

'Well, I don't feel well at all and Brian and Alan here have doubts about their effectiveness even if they can reach Camp 3.'

The exchange was punctuated by pauses waiting for the 'Over', to mark the end of one message. Only one party could speak at a time as the transmit button cut out sound reception. The tendency to interject comments into conversation as it went along was thus thwarted and in an crucial exchange like this there was much frustration in waiting to speak.

Ade said: 'If no one comes up to Camp 3 they won't ever get acclimatized to the altitude. It's best to come up and have a day's rest here if necessary instead of waiting at the Lho La to feel fit. That's 3,000 feet lower. Is anyone going to come or not?'

'The feeling here is that you are being over-optimistic'

'Look, we went up there yesterday specifically to find out and we reckon it is worth trying even in the wind if we are roped up.'

'Brian suggests that you and Joe go to establish Camp 4 if you think it possible, people can then come up to give a hand.'

'We need help now. We need at least the moral support of knowing that we aren't sticking our necks out going along that ridge, which won't be easy, only to find we've done it for nothing.'

'If you two doubt your ability to get along there, and you're going better than any of us, what chance has anyone else got?'

'Look it's black and white. We can't do everything on our own. If no one comes up there is no point in us going on.'

'Don't try to put the onus on us. If you want to give it a go getting to Camp 4 then do so.'

The artificially clipped manner of the dialogue also lent bluntness to the comments. With anyone else making this exchange there would have been the risk of arousing hostility by such sharp retorts. However, the anger which I knew Ade felt and which he was trying to express to his brother was curtailed by the formalities of radio talk. Ade swore for me to hear as his brother's mono-tone replies came out of the radio. There was a clear polarization between the two camps. Brian described the radio exchange as heard at Camp 1:

'The three of us, Alan, Al and myself, lay side by side in the ice cave, surrounded by a jumble of clothing and gear.

Alan was huddled up, his down-suited body protruding from his sleeping bag, a morose expression on his face. Al had the walkie-talkie in his hands. I broke into the exchange which Al was having with his brother: 'What the hell do they mean – need our support? What are we sat in this ice box for if it's not support? Let me talk to them, Al!'

'No, I just want to finish talking, to Ade. They must realize that there is no way we can get to the top now.'

I agreed with him: 'Yes, can't they see that with Paul and John on their way home, Pete with a broken rib, you with a bad chest, me and Alan totally demoralized, we just haven't got enough people left to make an attempt on the summit?'

Suddenly Alan burst out angrily. Give me the radio! Lho La to Camp 3, do you receive me? Over.'

'Ade from 3. Receiving at strength one. Please repeat. Over.'

Alan twiddled with knobs and the aerial before shouting into the radio and receiving Ade's reply. 'Receiving you strength four. If nobody will come up to help us we cannot continue. We need support. If you can't come up, we will come down. Over.'

Aside from the radio, Alan responded with more impatience: 'What the hell are they talking about? We've been sat here for seven days out of the last ten. We've had three good days in the last month when we could climb along the West Ridge. We need eight continuous days of good weather to get to the top. I'm bored with lying here day after day, feeling cold, ill and hungry.'

'Lho La to Camp 3, Alan here!' he shouted into the radio, pausing between each word so that the message was emphatic. 'If ... the ... weather ... gets ... better ... we ... will ... come ... up ... No ... point ... otherwise ... Just ... to ... get ... tired ... at ... Camp ... 3 ... You ... are ... only ... two ... strong

... enough ... to ... push ... above ... Camp ... 3 ... Over.'

Camp 3 to Lho La. Sorry, reception bad. Please repeat. Over.'

'If ... weather ... gets ... better ... will ... come ... up ... Over.'

With that, Alan's voice finally cracked and he croaked in a whisper: 'Oh Christ, somebody else try to get some sense out of them,' and he finished with a fit of coughing and retching.

Suddenly Pete broke in: 'Hello Camp 3 and Camp 1, Pete speaking from Base, can I add a few comments? Over.'

'Hearing you loud and clear ... Over.'

Pete continued: 'There seems to be a crucial discussion going on. I know I have got a broken rib but my vote is for pressing on. I'm not saying we can do it now at this late stage but I think we should stick it out for another few days. Things might just work out for us?'

I took the radio: 'Hello, Joe speaking. Those are my feelings too. Time is short but we might as well use it. We do need some support.'

Pete: 'Could you and Ade just stay up another few days?'

'We could stay up a few more days but I don't fancy sticking my neck out not knowing what is going on.'

'Can't you give a demonstration of what is still possible by going along to Camp 4? That might change the whole attitude.'

'We gave a bloody demonstration yesterday. What do you think this is, a circus? I don't think it's time for demonstrations. Everyone at Camp 1 seems to disagree that there's any chance left of us getting up the mountain in the weather we are stuck with now. If they can't get up now, what is the likelihood of them coming up in three days' time? We aren't putting the onus on them of calling a halt – the onus is on them. We are getting nowhere with this conversation. No one is, saying what they really mean. Before coming to any hasty decision, let's think about it. Let's have another radio call at eleven to give everyone time to think things over.'

We switched off. Ade and I relapsed into a glum silence. We both knew each other's minds. We wanted to go on even though we knew there remained little chance. The most rewarding achievements only come from succeeding against the greatest odds. On the other hand we had more than the weather to contend with. Ade and I had been lucky in escaping most of the ills which had bedevilled the expedition and when one is fit it is hard to comprehend how great problems can be, both mental and physical, for someone who is sick. There had been a lot of debilitating sickness and Everest in winter was showing no mercy to the sick. Brian had just recovered from yet another attack of dysentery. Alan, a skeleton of his former self, could hardly be understood over the radio, his voice was so hoarse, and now Al too had developed a chest infection. Sickness makes everything seem so much more difficult and even were it possible for anyone to drive himself on, the result could be fatal.

Ade was convinced that there would be no change of opinion. The date was 31 January. We had been on the mountain for nearly two months. The constant cold, bitter, brutal winds and snowstorms had steadily eroded our strength and resources. Perhaps Everest was too big an objective to tackle so early in this new phase of Himalayan exploration; the problems were far different and less obvious than in other seasons. I did feel in one part of my mind that there would be some relief in giving up this interminable struggle; the mental and physical strain of sustaining such effort over two months is extreme and no matter what the disappointment at not reaching the top there would be the pleasure of having survived, the satisfaction of knowing that we had battled with Everest at the worst time of the year and had not lost anyone or had any serious accidents.

While waiting for 11 a.m. and the decision, we made another drink and started sorting out which gear we would take down.

Outside only the eyes of an optimist could see the weather as being reasonable, and for the past month, apart from two days, we had known only storm and wind. There was no indication that we could expect any better in the next few days.

At 11 a.m. we opened up radio communication again.

'Hello Camp 1 and Base are you listening? What is the position now? Are there any new thoughts on the situation? Over.'

Pete came on the radio and there was a dialogue between him and Camp 1. Brian gave his view of it:

Pete's voice was enthusiastic, I could tell, even over the radio:

'Pete to Camp 1 and 3. I think that whilst we still have time left and people on the mountain we should keep trying at least for another week. Perhaps we'll get a spell of good weather. Can't anyone from Camp 1 get up to Camp 3? Over.'

I resented Pete sitting at Base Camp and trying to tell us what to do. 'Thanks, Pete, but winds are too strong today. Could not get up the ropes, but see no point in going up anyway if there is going to be just more bad weather.'

Alan sat up from a bout of coughing and, echoing my own and Al's sentiments, said into the radio: 'Get lost, Pete, you're just complicating things.'

Pete obviously did not hear this at Base Camp and Al commented after some thought: 'I suppose Pete's got just as much right to his opinion as everyone else.'

'Yes,' I said, 'it's just that discussing the end of a trip which you've worked on for the past six months, over a radio with poor reception, does not lend itself to friendly conversation.'

Joe's voice cut in with icy finality: 'If you don't come up from Camp 1 in support we might as well come down. Over.'

At Camp 3 we heard Al reply: 'If you want to stay up we are prepared to back you but there doesn't seem much point.'

'Is anyone coming up?'

'No one is really fit enough to.'

The refusal to come to the point and the oral fencing round the real issue continued. Ade groaned. He left the radio on 'receive' and we heard Pete come in again from Base Camp and conduct a long dialogue with Camp 1 on the same lines as the earlier discussion. 'To me,' Ade said: 'Nothing has changed. We might as well face it. They're never going to come up. By support we're talking about different things. I think they mean they'll be praying for us. They can't help being ill, but wait till I see our kid. I think this winter game has been too much for everyone.'

There was a look of resignation on his face and he started to stuff gear into a rucksack for descent. I lay back, listening to the discussion flying back and forth between Camp 1 and Base Camp. Pete was putting up a spirited argument for maintaining the impetus. The response from Camp 1 was that he was misjudging the situation on the mountain and that he himself was not of much use anyway with a broken rib. The discussion went on and on. Half an hour passed and Ade was ready to leave. The attitudes of everyone concerned were exactly the same as they had been at the start.

'There isn't going to be any change,' said Ade, I'm going to set off down. Might as well try and get to Base Camp in one go. See you later.' He pushed his sack up the tunnel and disappeared.

I too busied myself retrieving valuable pieces of camera gear and sleeping bags. When I was ready to leave I waited a while longer, listening to the still raging discourses. Still no change, and I scrambled up the tunnel for the last time, turning my thoughts to the consolations – no more grim nights in that hole, the gradual return to civilization and comfort.

My rucksack was exceedingly heavy. Both Ade and I were taking down the maximum possible knowing that that it was unlikely that anyone else would now be coming up. As I swung down the ropes on the steepening slopes back to the Lho La, I had to fight the wind throwing me off balance and I asked myself how realistic I had been in declaring that it would have been possible to make further progress in such weather. Did I really think we stood any chance now of getting up the mountain or did I simply not want to lose face by capitulating to a more rational assessment of our situation? I did not know the answer myself. The way down to the level plateau of the Lho La seemed interminable. I could see Ade, far below, and a tiny speck which left Camp 1 on its way down. I sank to my knees to rest at every anchor point, longing to be out of the wearying wind.

The plateau of the Lho La was only a change, not a relief. The wind knocked me back and forth and I paused frequently, waiting for a lull before staggering on a few steps. The final slight rise up to Camp 1 took forever. I felt self-conscious under the scrutiny of Alan who was waiting at the cave entrance with a drink ready.

Al had already gone down. Alan and Brian were staying at Camp 1 to pack everything up and clear as much gear as possible. Ade left as soon as I arrived and I hastened after him.

I dumped my sack halfway down as my legs kept giving way beneath me and once clear of the roped areas I knew I could easily retrieve it the next day. At the camp I walked into a barrage of questions by a camera and microphone from the film crew wanting instant reactions to the decision to call off the expedition.

Ade was involved in an angry dispute with his brother. 'Bloody support,' I heard him say 'You couldn't carry a shopping basket to a supermarket, let alone a sack of gear up this hill.' Al looked crestfallen and apologetic. Harder words could fly between these two than between any of the rest of us, and Ade was clearing his system of all the resentment that had built up over the last few days before the task of winding up the expedition should take precedence and form us into a working team again.

12   The Wind Up

Our postal system had finally shown a flaw. A mail bag had gone missing –
a multitude of letters and cards, ninety minutes of film, $300 in travellers'
cheques. We had sent the mail bag in question at the beginning of January and
it had taken a month for it to be reported to us that it had not arrived in
Kathmandu. None of us kept track of to whom we had written or when; that
mail was irretrievable. Mike Shrimpton, professional to the last, had a note of
every roll of film he had sent off, and dutifully he set off back up to the Lho La
to retake as much of the missing footage as he could. There was much coming
and going at this time retrieving gear from the mountain and Mike went up
with Brian and Pete. Pete showed an unsuspected propensity for conservation
even going back up to Camp 3 once to rescue what bits Ade and I had been unable to carry down. Some things were too bulky but rather than abandon them
Pete made a couple of large bundles and trundled them down the 3,000-foot
slope to the Lho La, rescuing the remains much later when he himself arrived.

The Japanese and Italians were also in the process of dismantling their Base
Camps. Hordes of porters and Sherpas arrived, invading our solitude and
picking like looters at every unattended piece of equipment or box of food.
They had long grown accustomed to expeditions winding up and abandoning
much valuable gear so that they have come to take it that they have a right to
anything left around. These were Sherpas in a different light from what we had
seen before and the camp had the feel of a beleaguered garrison as we cleared
up, burning rubbish and packing our belongings ready for departure.

Mr Singh became ill and did not appear from his tent for three days. The
only sound emanating from that direction was indistinguishable between
singing and groaning. Graham, camped beside him, reported hearing the same
sounds throughout the night and believed the strain of nearly three months
in the mountains was beginning to unbalance our shy Liaison Officer.

Finally we left, the familiar smell of juniper wood smoke from the Italian
camp trailing after us for a long time. The chaos of packing, loading yaks, argu-
ing over rates and weights, all compressed into a straggling line of ponderous
animals as we made our way downwards into deeper snow where the wind had
not blown with such force.

In only a short time Everest slipped behind the wall of Nuptse and our self-
imposed exile was over. I had a feeling of freedom, of walking unencumbered

by any constraints; alive again with no dangers ahead to face up to; alive with
dreams still intact, with a goal to aim for. This had been a punishing experience. We had kept in control, we were all returning without loss of life or limb
in the party, but in two months we had grown to accept as normal the most
harrowing living conditions we had known and had tried to climb the highest
mountain in the world by it's most difficult route. The Japanese, with a different style of expedition on a different route, had been turned back from a similar height on the same mountain. Some of our party thought that Everest,
in winter, without oxygen and especially by the West Ridge, was impossible.
The time needed to be spent on the mountain had left us weak and unable to
combat illnesses. The winds had been relentless and it was often physically
impossible to move in them. There was no doubt that we had every justifica-
tion in retreating before we found ourselves fighting for our lives with no physical or material resources left; But the objective remained. Perhaps we needed
this expedition to learn what was necessary for success. Few people dare to say
that any problem in mountaineering now is impossible to solve; failure only
enhances the prestige of the objective. After dropping somewhat in esteem in
recent years due to the numerous ascents of the mountain, Everest was now
restored to its pre-eminent position. Winter mountaineering in the Himalayas
opens a new chapter in the sport with the ascent of Everest as its greatest prize.

We made our way over several days to Lukla, the air strip from which we
were to fly out. The lower valleys, with trees laden with snow, had a more familiar look of winter than the Base Camp we had left where the barren wastes
change little with the arrival of more snow.

We met a Sherpa, 'Long' Tensing, who had been with the Burgess twins
on an earlier expedition: 'Success?'

'No.'

'Members all OK?'

'Yes.'

'On Everest that is success!'

In Kathmandu the pace of life changed. Months away from modern communications and we were like savages undergoing culture shock. The first night
back and we found ourselves at a party in an embassy house. They were all the
'beautiful people' of Kathmandu but we were ill at ease. Lost in the mêlée of
noise and strangers, we clung together for reassurance, unable to make conversation or relate to what was happening.

We were eating in a restaurant once when a shaven-headed girl, dressed in
the purple robes of the Buddhist faith, walked up to our table. She looked
from one Burgess twin to the other.

'Which one?' she said, and Al, his gaping mouth demonstrating his bewilderment, recognized the girl he had met on the way in.

The twins stayed behind to forward all our baggage. The rest of us, gradually separating off from the close-knit group we had become, boarded the plane for home. I was not prepared for it. A million strings were drawing me back but those strings came from another side of a wall and did not have any meaning until I should be amongst them again. As we approached London I felt a sense of nervousness as if I had become estranged from life at home and that back in the mountains we had left some unfinished business.

Acknowledgements

This is a personal account of the British Everest Winter Expedition. There are as many different facets to the story as there were people on the venture. However, in putting together this account, I received substantial contributions from Brian Hall, Allen Jewhurst, Paul Nunn, John Porter, Pete Thexton and Mike Shrimpton. I am indebted to Christopher Falkus of Eyre Methuen and George Greenfield of John Farquharson for their enthusiasm and Ann Mansbridge for her painstaking editorial work and rigorous discipline which kept me to a tight schedule. To my colleagues who made it possible to complete the book in the time available, and to Jill Hield who typed the manuscript with most helpful speed and efficiency, I owe a particular debt of gratitude.

Bass Ltd, New Era Laboratories, the Mount Everest Foundation and the British Mountaineering Council all provided financial support and many companies, particularly Mountain Equipment and Berghaus, provided material support, all of which made the expedition possible in the first place.

To these, and to the team above all, I owe thanks.

Joe Tasker
Hope, Derbyshire
1982

About the Author

Joe Tasker was one of Britain's foremost mountaineers. He was a pioneer of lightweight, 'Alpine-style' climbing in the Greater Ranges and had a special talent for writing. He died, with his friend Peter Boardman, high on Everest in 1982 while attempting the previously unclimbed North East Ridge. Their deaths marked the end of a remarkable era in British mountaineering.

Born in Hull in 1948, Joe began rock climbing in his teens. Drawn to mountaineering, he made many remarkable ascents in the Alps, including the first British winter ascent of the North Face of the Eiger, before moving to the Greater Ranges. Here, Joe pioneered routes of extreme technical difficulty in a bold, Alpine-style – at a time when huge expeditions and siege tactics were still the mountaineering norm.

Peter and Joe left two legacies. One was their great endeavour, their climbs on high peaks with bold, lightweight innovative methods; the second is the books they wrote and left behind. Both had developed a special talent for writing. Joe's first book *Everest the Cruel Way* is an exciting account of his winter attempt on Everest and his second book, *Savage Arena*, was finished just before he left for Everest in 1982. Both have become mountaineering classics.

The Boardman Tasker Prize for Mountain Literature was established in Pete and Joes' honour, and is presented annually to the author or co-authors of an original work which has made an outstanding contribution to mountain literature. For more information about the Boardman Tasker Prize, visit: *www.boardmantasker.com*

LAYAH HEILPERN

UNDRESSING
BITCOIN

A Revealing Guide To The Wo

G000016920

UNDRESSING BITCOIN

A Revealing Guide To The World's Most Revolutionary
Asset

LayahHeilpern

DISCLAIMER

Nothing in this book should be taken as financial advice.

Everything in this book is my opinion, based on my experience in the cryptocurrency industry so far. I am not a financial advisor; please always contact a qualified professional financial advisor before making any decisions. This book is not sponsored by any companies mentioned.

DEDICATION

This book is dedicated to my brother, Gideon Heilpern, who has supported and guided me through my career so far.

INTRODUCTION

Unless you've been living under a rock, and avoiding all forms of social media and financial news, you've definitely heard of a new reality that has completely disrupted the traditional monetary system. This "new reality", often referred to by insiders as "magic internet money", was born out of the dereliction of duty by our world leaders. Perhaps you ignored it for a while, or maybe you even attempted to understand and invest but found it complicated and secretive. For a while, this "new reality" seemed to be an exclusive club, with many outsiders banging on the door, desperate to get in on this technological and philosophical revolution. Before we begin this journey, I would like to highlight three extremely significant values of this "magic internet money": sovereignty, decentralisation and individual responsibility. These core values are entrenched in the revolution that is BITCOIN!

CONTENTS

CHAPTER 1

The Death Of Fiat Currency

Welcome To Undressing Bitcoin

———•◦◇◦•———

You may be wondering why we desperately need an alternative system. Everything surrounding your relationship with the current monetary system probably feels natural and stable. In this environment, you might have a successful job with a well-paying salary, and perhaps you're even saving some money for a "rainy day". Authority figures in our lives such as teachers, parents and political leaders have told us: if we go to school, get a degree and work hard enough, we will get ourselves on the esteemed property ladder. And perhaps if you're lucky enough, one day you could retire and finally enjoy the fruits of your labour.

We've all heard the expression, "if it ain't broke, don't fix it", so why is there a growing movement advocating for a shift from the traditional financial system, to something entirely new? So let's start at the very beginning, exposing how and why the traditional financial system is obsolete and broken.

Before I discuss the advocacy for an alternative system, I'd like to introduce you to the scam, I mean the term "fiat", pronounced like the Italian car company. Fiat currency is a government and central bank-issued currency, like the U.S. Dollar, Pound Sterling, or Euro. Moreover, fiat currencies have no intrinsic value, and some might argue the "perceived" value comes from the government's promise to maintain and stabilise the country's currency and economy.

There are three predominant built-in bugs with the current financial system: absolute tyranny through centralisation, hyperinflation and mass manipulation. As I discuss in further detail and take you on this BITCOIN journey, I hope to provide you with a new perspective on money, and why we urgently need a technological and philosophical revolution, in the form of BITCOIN!

Money has been a part of our society for at least 3,000 years, dating back to when people used gold as a medium of exchange for goods and services. Due to the fact gold is highly valuable and not practical to carry around, goldsmiths would charge customers to store their gold in vaults. Subsequently, the goldsmiths provided paper receipts representing gold holdings, which in turn were traded in the marketplace to buy and sell goods and services. This is where the concept of legal tender, also known as paper currency, and modern banking emanates from.

Fast forward to the beginning of the 20th century: the U.S. passed The Gold Standard Act, which meant gold was the only precious metal that could be exchanged for paper currency. When the U.S. Dollar is directly linked to the value of gold, central banks, which control a country's monetary policy, cannot increase the money supply without increasing the amount of gold held in reserves. As a result of the Gold Standard, the value of the U.S. Dollar was directly linked to the value of gold, but to the U.S. Dollar's detriment, this was abolished in 1971.

Why Was The Gold Standard Abolished?

In the 1930s the infamous Great Depression in the United States brought the economy to a halt. And in order to stimulate the economy, the government made a "brilliant" decision to print more money than gold held in reserves. This may have temporarily stabilised the economy, however, it also greatly damaged the value of the U.S. Dollar long term.

From the Great Depression up until the 1970s, the U.S. began to sell its gold reserves to foreign governments in exchange for the U.S. Dollar. This drastically depleted America's gold reserves, and in 1971 President Nixon abolished the Gold Standard, bringing an end to an era where the value of the U.S. Dollar was backed by the gold held in reserves.

What Is The Dollar Backed By Now?

In 2021 the U.S. Dollar is backed by treasury securities such as bonds, bills and notes, and these securities are essentially debt obligations of the U.S. government. In layman's terms, the Dollar is backed by debt, and according to my values, debt-backed money doesn't inspire too much faith. This is why you will often hear the general claim, "the Dollar is not backed by anything at all". Ultimately, the Dollar is backed by our faith that the government will repay the debt, and on that note, I'd like to share a quote from PayPal in 2021:

"Fiat currency is a government-issued currency that is not backed by a physical commodity, such as gold or silver, but rather by the government that issued it."

Let's go to the notorious 2008/9 financial crisis which is an extremely significant point in time, as BITCOIN was largely born out of the catastrophe that surrounded it. As you can imagine, the financial crisis s a complex topic, and to be frank extremely dull and boring, just like the people in it. However, I'd like to very briefly explain the overall failures of the traditional system, so you can understand why the case for BITCOIN is so imperative.

The banks and major institutions on Wall Street and around the world overexposed themselves and took too many financial risks. This directly caused a financial crisis, with mass unemployment, debt and in some cases poverty. The very people the banks stole money from (the taxpayers, thanks very much!) ended up bailing out the banks to the sum of $850 billion, which in many cases is still going on to this day!

Inflation

From the very first day I heard about BITCOIN, I've had a burning desire to share the truth and everything I have learnt through my personal experiences. To kick things off, inflation is the hidden tax that the majority of people either fail to understand, or more concerningly have never even heard of, thanks largely to our obsolete education system. Inflation is predominantly caused by Quantitative Easing (Q.E.), which is a deceptive way of concealing the truth behind printing endless amounts of money and pumping it into an economy. Prior to the abolishment of the Gold Standard, the government was unable to cause inflation to a large extent, as increasing the Dollar supply was not possible. However, since the abolishment of the Gold Standard, printing and pumping money into an economy has become as common as the cold in today's economies.

Pandemic

Between March 2020 and March 2021, the enslavement machine, or more commonly known as the Federal Reserve, or the central banking system of the U.S., pumped more than $9 trillion into the economy. This means more than 22% of the U.S. Dollar in circulation was printed in 2020 alone; just let that sink in for a moment. Since the birth of BITCOIN 12 years ago, 75% of the total U.S. Dollar supply has been printed, devaluing the currency and purchasing power to the lowest point in history.

Here's another great statistic for you: the enslavement machine, I mean the Federal Reserve, generally increases the Dollar supply by 5% every year. However, by 2021 this figure rose to an outstanding 40%. Wow at this rate America's greasy buffalo wings and Wendy's hamburgers are going to get really expensive.

In March 2020, Jerome Powell, the Chairman of the Federal Reserve, sat down for an interview to discuss this exact topic.

The interviewer asked, "Is it fair to say you simply flooded the system with money?"

To which Powell responded, "Yes we did, that's another way to think about it."

Interviewer: "Where does it come from? Do you just print it?"

Powell: "We print it digitally, as a central bank we have the ability to create money…"

This Powell guy must think we are a bunch of foolish sheep, perhaps he is right?

Why Will Those Buffalo Wings and Wendy's Hamburgers Get Really Expensive?

The problem with increasing the money supply comes down to simple economics. By printing money and therefore increasing the circulating supply, you greatly reduce the purchasing power of the currency. Apply these economics to the U.S. Dollar or the Great British Pound, and you will see the money in your pocket decrease in value over time, eventually becoming worthless. This is called inflation.

To help illustrate inflation, I always like to use my grandfather as an example. In the 1960s he bought his house in England for £2,500, and as of 2021, his house is worth approximately £250,000. Despite his property being what appears to be a viable investment and hedge against inflation, I will demonstrate how our money has been burnt over time.

With the average wage of £728 per annum in the 60s, and the average UK house price of £2,500, one would have to save for 3.5 years in order to *cash purchase* a property; note I said *cash purchase* meaning the absence of a mortgage. In 2021, the average wage is £29,600 per annum, and the average UK house price is £250,000. In today's inflated world, one would have to save for a much greater 8.5 years, in order to cash purchase the same property. My example demonstrates as time goes on the purchasing power of our money decreases and we have to work harder and longer hours to afford a living. Failure to adopt an alternative system (hello BITCOIN) will result in a far lower quality of life, and the inevitable enslavement to government central banks.

£700 For A Loaf Of Bread! Welcome To Hyperinflation In Venezuela

The strength and stability of the Venezuelan Bolivar is predicated on the country's oil exports. As global oil prices fell drastically in 2014, the demand for the Bolivar plummeted, spiralling the economy into crisis. In order to repair and stabilise the economy, President Nicolas Maduro's government decided it would be a brilliant idea to print more money. Subsequently, this skyrocketed inflation to a ludicrous 80,000%. To give you some context, if this level of hyperinflation happened in the United Kingdom, it would be the equivalent of paying £1,475 for two loaves of bread. Well done to President Nicolas Maduro for impoverishing your entire nation.

The frightening reality of it all is how quickly a once-prosperous Venezuela, exporting oil all around the world, suddenly crashed to its doom. This is why we should always be aware of the catastrophe and downfall that manifests when central banks print money from thin air. But what if there was a currency that had a fixed supply, and a monetary policy that wasn't dictated by a centralised authority? What if the currency was democratic, run by the people, and immune to manipulation from central banks and governments? What if the currency had built-in mechanisms that allowed it to become scarcer over time?

Enter BITCOIN

The origin of BITCOIN is not entirely known, however, it's widely accepted that it was created by a person or group of individuals that go by the pseudonym Satoshi Nakomoto.

The objective was to create money not backed by debt, and a system that is similar to democracy ruled by the people and for the people only. BITCOIN is implicitly decentralised, it is impossible for a central authority to directly interfere and manipulate the network. BITCOIN is often referred to as a "peaceful protest", because when you adopt the new technology, you are peacefully choosing to opt- out of a declining and obsolete system that no longer has your best interests at heart. Furthermore, by doing so you are indirectly boycotting the central bank and the wider establishment.

BITCOIN is considered by its community to be the scarcest and most valuable asset in the world, especially when considering the fixed supply of only twenty-one million coins ever available. Another reason BITCOIN is considered the most valuable asset in the world is due to the real-world use cases and problems the network is solving on a daily basis. Now that's out of the way and you have some context, it's time to undress Bitcoin and find out how sexy this thing really is.

CHAPTER 2

The Elegance And Sophistication Of The Bitcoin Network

————•o◇o•————

BITCOIN is a peer-to-peer digital currency that has no central authority and allows two people to transact directly, without going through any form of third party intermediary like a bank. BITCOIN has a fixed and limited supply of twenty-one million coins, and no more will ever be created. However, not all twenty-one million coins have been released, so grab yours while you can. In the event somehow additional BITCOINs are created, this would simply no longer be considered BITCOIN, which I will expand on later.

The physical laws for the Bitcoin network are enshrined in the Holy Grail that is the whitepaper. The whitepaper comprises the laws on how the network is secured and maintained through the technology. Think of it like this: the whitepaper is the modern 10 commandments that God gave to Moses; it's that important and valuable.

BITCOIN operates on the Bitcoin network, which essentially is one big computer network all around the world, and is therefore appropriately referred to as a decentralised blockchain-based system. This system is maintained and secured by decentralised computers that are run by people known as "miners". Essentially, it's one global ledger system, whereby the miners confirm the transactions that you and I make. Once the transactions are confirmed, miners add the information onto the blockchain; this is known as a new "block". To give you some context the genesis block was the first BITCOIN block to be mined in 2009, recognising a significant moment in history and the start of an era.

The blockchain is a string of blocks that contains a record of every single transaction on the Bitcoin network. The blockchain is a public ledger, available for anyone around the world to view, adding further accountability to the network. Now, doesn't that sound incredibly free, transparent and perhaps refreshing? This is why the system is often referred to as "trustless", due to the absence of a single authority regulating and controlling the network. Subsequently, we get one of my favourite terms from the BITCOIN community: "Don't trust, VERIFY!" This is the exact opposite of a bank's centralised ledger of transactions, which requires our full moral and ethical trust in an institution. I personally don't trust my own family with my passwords and pin numbers, so why would I trust a bunch of self-serving corporations and tyrannical governments?

BITCOIN was created to secure a certain level of privacy for its users, as part of BITCOIN's core values is individual responsibility and sovereignty, which is impossible to attain with centralisation; the two are not compatible. There's an important distinction to highlight between anonymity and traceability. One of BITCOIN's core values is to be simultaneously anonymous whilst traceable. A BITCOIN address, which is the equivalent of your bank details, has a high level of anonymity, as the address is not associated with any personal details, such as a name. However, a simple online search of a respective BITCOIN address can reveal the quantity of money held and previous transactional history.

Miners

Miners are one of the most important pieces of the puzzle, not to be confused with the old men working in tunnels. Welcome to the 21st-century version! In order to secure the network, miners undertake a job called proof-of-work and are rewarded with newly minted BITCOINs, known as the block reward. As of 2021, each miner receives 6.25 BITCOIN, plus a share of the transaction fees. Given that one BITCOIN is in the tens of thousands, getting paid 6.25 BITCOIN sounds pretty good, right? Well, not entirely, mining BITCOIN consists of large expenses including the mining machinery and the electricity costs to operate them.

The block rewards allow the Bitcoin network to be secured by a decentralised *incentive model*. Miners are incentivised to do their job correctly and efficiently, as any disruption or fraudulent activity will result in miners not receiving their block rewards. This infuses faith and confidence into the network and provides a common objective, irrespective of religion, gender, or ethnicity. For a further layer of security, anyone around the world can choose to run a system called a "node", which means holding a copy of the Bitcoin blockchain to further decentralise and secure the network. In conclusion, the entire system has full congruence, as everyone hosting and facilitating the network has a direct interest in maintaining and securing the Bitcoin blockchain.

Proof-Of-Work

Now for the infamous, and yes indeed the infamous, proof-of-work consensus mechanism. POW is the core technological mechanism that miners use to confirm and validate transactions, and in fact what makes Bitcoin the most secure network in the world. When sending BITCOIN, the transaction is added to an unconfirmed transaction pool, called a memory pool or "mempool" for short. To keep this as simple as possible as it can become extremely complex: miners essentially compete against each other to confirm the transaction, by racing to decode a string of characters, which is known as finding the "nonce". Once a miner has successfully found the nonce, they are responsible for adding the new block to the blockchain. Other miners around the world are required to confirm the work has been completed correctly, and that everyone is sharing the same copy of the blockchain. This is why it's called proof-of-work, as miners are literally proofing the work. POW requires a great deal of complex computational energy, which is why miners are rewarded with BITCOIN. Often people will refer to POW as a "trial and error process", because miners use machines to generate these random codes needed to "win" and add the new block to the blockchain.

The Heartbeat Of BITCOIN

Think of this as a human, BITCOIN's heartbeat pumps at an average of seven transactions per second, and a new block is added to the blockchain approximately every ten minutes.

Conserving these rules is vital in ensuring the health of the network and maintaining the supply and demand of the currency, as scarcity is one of the most significant characteristics that gives BITCOIN its value.

So what if BITCOIN's heartbeat sped up to 14 transactions per second, due to miners solving the trial and error process faster and more efficiently? This could result in more BITCOINs on the market than expected, therefore temporarily having a negative impact on its price. Therefore, in order to counter this likely possibility, a unique and exquisite algorithm exists called the difficulty adjustment. This works similar to a pacemaker, ensuring the blocks are adhering to the ten-minute new block schedule, exemplifying the self-regulation of the network.

If blocks are added to the chain too quickly or even too slowly, the difficulty adjustment is triggered, altering the complexity level of the trial and error process. This makes it either easier or harder to solve, depending on what is necessary to ensure the correct ten- minute block schedule. This is an algorithmic defence mechanism with the sole purpose of managing inflation.

Can BITCOIN Reach Half A Million?! The Halving

With all the loud sound bites and price predictions we've heard, is it entirely possible for BITCOIN to reach half a million dollars? Especially when considering the community constantly forecasts extravagant figures all over Twitter and the wider internet. Well, it might be possible through Bitcoin's built-in scarcity mechanism, known as the halving event. The halving event or the "halvening" is a genius event that occurs after 210,000 blocks are mined, approximately every four years.

During the halving event, the block rewards are cut in half, as a way of ensuring BITCOIN's scarcity. As the approximate four-year halving cycle occurs, less BITCOIN is supplied to the market. The idea being, with less BITCOIN released, the price will steadily increase, making it a deflationary asset. Given this is precisely the opposite of inflation and money printing, you can imagine Bitcoin's deflationary components must be giving the establishment nightmares.

As an example, at the time of writing, the most recent halving event took place in May 2020, where the reward was cut in half, from 12.5 BITCOINs per block to 6.25. The halving cycle will continue until all twenty-one million BITCOINs have been mined. Therefore it's estimated the block reward will reach its limit around the year 2140.

So what happens in the year 2140, and how will miners be incentivised to continue securing the network? This is an interesting question considering everyone asking will not be alive to find out. The most sufficient and widely accepted answer is, by

2140 miners will be compensated through transaction fees, which will have significantly increased due to the block reward reaching its limit. Furthermore, the network will continue to maintain itself the same way, through its incentivised system.

FAKE BITCOIN: The Double-Spend Problem

The double-spend problem was one of the biggest complications that digital currencies faced in the 90s, and refers to the risk of duplicate and fraudulent transactions. The fundamental problem is that electronic files can easily be duplicated. For example, an e- ticket simply requires the original owner to forward the ticket via email to another person; consequently, two tickets now exist, despite only one ticket initially bought. This was a huge concern with digital currencies developed in the 80s and a fundamental reason for their failure in the 90s.

One of BITCOIN's main objectives through its genius proof-of-work mechanism, is to ensure duplication of the currency is an impossibility. Once BITCOIN is sent from one party to another it enters a mempool. However, if the same BITCOIN is sent twice by the same person, both transactions will enter the pool and wait to be confirmed. Whichever transaction is removed first by the miners will be confirmed and added to the blockchain. However, once the duplicate transaction is removed, it will not be validated, as the miners have proof that the previous BITCOIN was removed and confirmed. It's also extremely important to realise, once BITCOIN has been sent to a specific address, it is absolutely irreversible. And failing to put the correct recipient address will result in loss of funds forever. In essence, unlike a traditional bank, there's no Karen running the HR department at BITCOIN. So you might want to take some responsibility.

Now you have an understanding of the basic fundamental technology behind BITCOIN, I'd like to discuss the individual responsibility that comes with holding and storing your BITCOIN. In a world saturated with professional cyber hackers and imposters, it's imperative to know what you're doing. It can be a dangerous world, so I'm going to show you how to armour up.

CHAPTER 3

How Not To Lose $50,000,000 In BITCOIN

———◦◇◦———

I want to start with one of BITCOIN's main philosophical values, individual sovereignty and autonomy. These philosophical values inspire a refreshing monetary system that empowers individuals to become self-sovereign, with the absence of centralised authority. Banksters, I mean banks, have the authority to freeze your funds unnecessarily and have the power to impose restrictions and limitations on your personal spending capacity. Furthermore, as we saw with the financial crisis, in a worst-case scenario banksters can engage in casino banking with customer deposit accounts.

I'm going to share an example of the worst personal experience I recently had the pleasure of encountering with a modern fintech bank. Prior to this experience, I held a respective personal and business account with large amounts of funds. I was under the impression everything would be safe and secure in their custody due to the Financial Conduct Authority (FCA) regulating them. However, as my funds grew, this fintech bank made an out of the blue request for proof of funds, so naturally, I obliged and sent all relevant documents. Despite the fintech bank receiving everything I could possibly give, they decided to freeze my respective accounts. At which point I had big bills to pay, such as rent, and this caused huge stress and aggravation. All the while the only explanation I received was the following: "This is a standard procedure and should be solved relatively soon." After a traumatic three weeks, my respective accounts were finally unfrozen and I was able to access my funds again.

Thankfully a large portion of my capital was deployed into BITCOIN, therefore I was able to use those funds to pay the necessary bills, avoiding further aggravation. Hopefully, now you understand the case for a monetary system that provides and encourages individual sovereignty, through decentralisation.

So how was I able to survive on BITCOIN, despite my traditional funds being locked? It's simple; I hold my BITCOIN in something called a non-custodial wallet. This means the funds are in my sole possession and no third party or authority has the power to freeze my BITCOIN. Here's how it works:

Where To Store Your Millions In BITCOIN

Since we're all going from rags to riches, where on earth are we going to store our fortunes safely and securely?

To send, receive and hold BITCOIN a digital "wallet" with a specific address is required, and anyone with an internet connection can create one. Essentially a wallet is a device or programme that enables you to access and control your

BITCOIN. I'm going to discuss the two main types of wallets: custodial and non-custodial, of which both kinds can either be a hot or cold wallet.

Imagine a BITCOIN wallet like a regular tangible wallet or purse, which sits in your pocket and holds your cash. A BITCOIN wallet is precisely this, however, it's digital and can be on your phone, computer, or portable device. Just to clarify, did you know cryptocurrencies are not actually stored inside the digital wallet? Cryptocurrencies in fact live on their respective blockchains, and therefore a wallet is merely a door to access your funds.

Essentially, your millions in BITCOIN are cryptographically locked away requiring two types of keys and one vital seed phrase for access.

The two kinds of keys given to access your BITCOIN are private and public keys and comprise a specific long string of numbers and letters. The numbers and characters on both keys appear to be almost identical, however as they serve entirely different purposes, it's imperative to distinguish the difference and not mix them up. The private key is a master key for accessing BITCOIN, and if someone obtains the private key, they can effectively deplete all your funds. It is your individual responsibility to safeguard the private key and never divulge this information to anyone. On the other hand, the public key is precisely the opposite, for example, in order to receive BITCOIN, you must provide the sender with your public key.

In the event you lose your private key, an alternative recovery phrase, known as the "seed phrase" is necessary to restore your funds and works as a master backup. The seed phrase typically contains a combination of 12 to 24 random words and should also be safeguarded and never divulged to anyone. For example, if your BITCOIN wallet is held on your phone and you decide to get a new one, the seed phrase is required to recover the previous wallet. Now that I've established that a wallet only acts as a door to the blockchain, it's important to be aware that some doors can be safer than others.

Custodial Wallets

A custodial wallet is when your BITCOIN is held by a third party, such as a cryptocurrency exchange like Binance and Coinbase. When BITCOIN is held in custody, this arrangement is similar to holding fiat currency with banksters, I mean banks, I just can't tell the difference at this point! Essentially, you're not directly in control over your funds, as they are held in trust, which creates potential exposure to counterparty risks and fraud.

Custodial wallets do not provide access to private keys or seed phrases, unlike non-custodial wallets. This is a simple and appropriate way to distinguish the difference between the two. A widely known phrase within the BITCOIN community to delineate the potential risk and exposure of custodial wallets is the following: "Not your keys, not your coins." Don't forget this!

Fraud And Hackers

Crypto custodians unfortunately can be susceptible to cyber hackers, despite how reputable and sophisticated an exchange may be. Often, it can become a matter of time before either the exchange or your personal account is hacked. In reality, an exchange holding your funds in trust is merely protected by a public email address and password; even online banking is required to enforce more security than this.

The Japanese BITCOIN exchange Mt. Gox and the Canadian exchange QuadrigaCX are well-known reported examples that you can research. Fundamentally speaking, thousands of customers collectively lost hundreds of millions in assets due to counterparty risk and fraud. Nevertheless, in the catastrophic event of an exchange hack, your funds could potentially be reimbursed. For example, in 2018 the leading cryptocurrency exchange Binance had 7,000 BITCOINs stolen, which at the time was worth $40 million (at the peak of 2021 this equated to $427M). Despite the enormity of this cyber hack, Binance covered the entire loss and reimbursed every customer wallet. However, this level of customer insurance is certainly not guaranteed and you should always proceed with caution when dealing with custodial platforms.

Non-Custodial Wallets And The Gateway To Financial Freedom

The gateway to financial freedom is to become self-sovereign and have full control and ownership over your assets. In my opinion, this truly is the core philosophy behind BITCOIN, and in these unprecedented times is certainly a solution to the impending enslavement by the system. In order to attain this level of sovereignty and financial freedom, you need to take self-custody of your assets, and a non-custodial wallet is how you go about this. Holding your BITCOIN in this capacity empowers you to truly own your assets, as you are the sole gatekeeper of your wallet, private keys and seed phrases. Unlike my experience with the fintech bank when my assets were frozen for three weeks, it is impossible for the funds in your non-custodial wallet to be frozen or liquidated by a third party. This is why holding your BITCOIN in a non-custodial wallet is considered the safest and most secure method of storage.

The two kinds of non-custodial wallets are software and hardware wallets. Software wallets are basically, as the name suggests, a piece of software like an app on your phone or computer. Exodus Wallet is an example of this and is typically referred to as "hot storage" since it's likely to be connected to the internet. However, as software wallets are usually connected to the internet through your phone or computer, there is always a potential risk of exposure to cyber hackers.

The Superlative Form Of Security

Now after you've stored your millions of dollars in BITCOIN in a non-custodial wallet, believe it or not there are further precautions you can take to ensure professional hackers and tyrannical governments have no chance of interfering with your funds. In order to attain the highest level of stealth, you must employ the ultimate form of security known as a hardware wallet. This is largely regarded as the crypto industry's bulletproof method of storage and is also known as cold storage as the funds are secured offline. The most popular brands available on the market are Ledger and Tezor, and both are small physical devices that appear similar to a USB stick. These devices are secured with a pin and require a connection to an app on your computer to transfer funds.

A common question of concern that's constantly echoed is "What happens if you lose your cold storage device or your device breaks?" In the event the device breaks, your

BITCOIN is not lost or frozen since your funds aren't stored inside the device. Remember, wallets are merely the door and gateway to your BITCOIN which is stored on the immutable blockchain. So long as you have your private key and seed phrase, you can always restore your wallet on another device.

Lost or Stolen?!

In the unfortunate event your device is lost or stolen you must immediately get a replacement device to mitigate against potential financial loss. Once you've restored your wallet on the new device, it will be active on both the replacement and old device. At which point you must immediately send your funds to a new address before your old device is found with your assets potentially drained. As far as the crypto community is aware, no one has had their funds hacked or digitally stolen by using a hardware wallet. In fact, the rare scenarios where individuals have lost their BITCOIN are usually a result of irresponsible self-custody of keys, seed phrases or the misplacement of the device.

Here are a few high-level security practices for you:

- **Do not write down your private key or seed phrase on a piece of paper, because paper can be easily destroyed. Consider using a metal sheet that can be engraved.**
- **Do not take a picture or screenshot of your keys on your phone as it's connected to the internet which defeats the purpose of cold storage.**
- **Do not change the order of the private key or seed phrase.**
- **Before sending all your BITCOIN to your cold wallet, send a nominal amount as a precautionary test. Once received, you may send the remainder.**

It's perfectly reasonable to use both a hardware and software wallet, as they can serve different purposes. Given that hardware wallets require a computer to gain access and make transfers, they can be rather impractical for daily use and better for long- term savings and security. Consequently, it is more efficient to leave a small amount of funds in a software wallet to make daily transactions, as this is accessible in real-time.

Ultimately, taking self-custody requires a lot of individual responsibility, and can be overwhelming for new adopters. If you're considering holding your BITCOIN on a centralised custodial exchange, make sure you are fully armoured up and have a form of two-factor authentication (2FA). Companies such as Google and Microsoft provide this extra layer of armour. Another example of extra security is the YubiKey, which is a small physical plug-in device that works as a key giving you access to your account. Now you know how to armour up and secure yourself, we can move on to the deeper philosophy of BITCOIN.

CHAPTER 4

Why BITCOIN Matters

Now we have a comprehension of the technological mechanisms, the time has come to show you this is not the only place BITCOIN derives value from. Welcome to the most thought-provoking and captivating chapter of Undressing Bitcoin.

This chapter provides a more philosophical perspective, enlightening you on the humanitarian case for BITCOIN. In the modern world, poverty remains a huge problem, despite all the efforts from private charities and governments, and for the first time, BITCOIN presents a unique solution to this long-lasting problem. Furthermore, with crony capitalism very much alive, tech giants and other major corporations finally face real competition through BITCOIN's decentralisation, bringing power back to the people.

The Financial Map

The financial map refers to an individual or a country's potential capacity to undertake business with the rest of the world. From the first moment I heard of BITCOIN, I immediately fell in love with its ability to lift people out of poverty, bringing them onto the financial map. Certain regions such as Africa and Latin America are deprived of the financial infrastructure predominantly seen in the West, consequently, a simple task such as opening a bank account is nearly impossible. Typically, banking facilities are either unavailable for miles or the individuals do not have the official documentation required to open an account, and are therefore ostracised from the rest of the world.

The World Bank data illustrates that 66% of sub-Saharan Africans are listed as unbanked. Nevertheless, the Global System for Mobile Communications demonstrated sub-Saharan Africa will have over one billion smartphone users by 2024. This is where BITCOIN as a humanitarian solution comes into effect. The one billion smartphone users will finally have the ability to build and create wealth, by simply downloading an app on their phone in seconds and opening a wallet to securely store their money. This effectively emancipates impoverished people, as they now have the opportunity to offer labour, goods and services both domestically and globally to more developed countries. The international labour market creates an opportunity to receive higher wages than they would typically receive domestically and also makes them more competitive in the global job market.

Traditional banks often require a minimum amount to execute an international transfer, however, those in developing regions typically cannot meet the requirements, as wages are very low. With this new modern and disruptive technology, micropayments are now possible, allowing everyone to build wealth, prosper economically and elevate themselves out of the cycle of poverty. In reality, Africa is the truest pioneer of this technology due to its less economically developed environment, and unlike the West it is skipping industrial revolutions, going straight to the 4th era of modern smart technology.

Decentralisation

The beauty in BITCOIN is the unprecedented decentralised network on which it thrives and operates. There is absolutely no central authority such as a government, corporation or a form of administration controlling or regulating the network. Decentralisation is the precise characteristic that makes BITCOIN so unique and attractive in a world of ever-growing tyranny and centralisation.

I want to share a story with you, which will make you realise the urgent case for a decentralised system. In early 2021, users on the social media platform Reddit went to war against large and influential hedge fund managers on Wall Street. Retail and amateur investors communicate through a specific Reddit forum called WallstreetBets. The community discuss highly speculative trades and engage in gallows humour as they believe the stock market is fixed and rigged like a game against them.

The retail and amateur investors recognised that Wall Street fund managers would constantly form alliances, with the purpose of shorting stocks and wrecking companies in order to profit in the billions. In this case, GameStop (GME) and AMC were the chosen companies Wall Street undertook short positions against. However, WallstreetBets strategically planned to do the opposite and executed long positions, skyrocketing the price of the stocks costing Wall Street institutions a huge loss of $70 billion.

Despite retail investors on Reddit beating Wall Street at their own game, unfortunately, their success was not long-lived. Here's where it gets ugly. The trading platform Robinhood in 2016 made an infamous tweet that captured their mission statement: "Let the people trade". However, in early 2021 Robinhood did precisely the opposite, barring retail investors from buying GME and AMC stock. Consequently, the Reddit community were unable to continue pumping the price; effectively their leverage was removed, disarming them against the big players. This specifically benefited the millions of dollars in short positions taken by Wall Street institutions.

The CEO of Robinhood, Vladimir Tenev, appeared on several major American news networks to clarify the decision. Unfortunately, people were none the wiser and rumours began to surface that Robinhood was colluding with Wall Street, and with just a few phone calls from influential CEOs they were able to put an end to WallstreetBets. This is only speculation and to this day we still don't know whether Robinhood deliberately barred retail investors from buying stock. Nevertheless, irrespective of the purpose behind Robinhood's decision, this is a classic example of the power and control that comes through centralisation.

In a truly decentralised system, there are no executive decision- makers, no cancel culture or de-platforming and decisions are always democratised. BITCOIN and the entire crypto space is a free market that anyone can get involved in. Furthermore, decentralisation is the precise module that makes the network almost impossible to cyber hack; I use the words "almost impossible" as nothing in life is certain. With nodes and miners distributed all around the world, there is no central or single point of failure or entry to attack. Decentralisation ensures that miners have one common objective, to see BITCOIN prosper.

You may have heard of the term "51% attack" which refers to a group of potential miners colluding to attack the network. Given how expensive BITCOIN is to mine, controlling more than 50% of the network will cost an extortionate amount of money. This is why an attack of this kind, or any cyber hack for that matter, has not yet occurred and is almost impossible.

The 7 Characteristics Of Viable Money The Government Doesn't Want You To Know

1. Scarcity/Limited supply
2. Durability
3. Portability
4. Divisibility
5. Uniformity
6. Fungibility
7. Acceptability

Scarcity

Scarcity is the most significant characteristic from where BITCOIN derives its value, as there will only ever be twenty-one million coins minted by the year 2140. In order to go beyond this limited supply, it would cause a fork in the network and any new coins minted would no longer be BITCOIN, but rather an entirely new network with its own coin. To put the significance of 21 million into perspective, there are seven billion people on this planet and only 21 million of them will ever have an opportunity to own a whole coin. This amounts to a microscopic 0.3%, so get yours while you can!

Due to BITCOIN's limited supply and store of value, it is often compared to gold and widely regarded as an alternative, becoming the ultimate hedge against inflation. However, gold does not have a finite supply like BITCOIN. A report from Fitch Solutions estimated that gold production would increase annually, by 2.5%, consequently supplying the market to a point of saturation. Furthermore, there is always more gold to be mined from the ground, the ocean and even from space. According to NASA, there's enough gold on an asteroid to make everyone on earth a billionaire. On the other hand, approximately every four years the amount of BITCOIN supplied to the market is cut in half, known as the halving event I spoke about in chapter 2. This is why BITCOIN is referred to as "digital gold" or "gold 2.0" and for the 100th time, there will only ever be 21 million coins minted.

Durability

The durability characteristic refers to how abrasive to physical deterioration money can be over a given lifespan. No one wants to receive money that is damaged or unrecognisable from "wear and tear", as this can make it valueless. For example, washing your clothes with paper money in the pockets will cause damage, giving a whole new meaning to the term money laundering. Despite some currencies being issued in plastic, money can still be set on fire, destroyed, or defaced. Ideally, money that withstands the test of time is what we want. When it comes to BITCOIN withstanding the test of time from a durability perspective, this concern is completely impertinent. Since BITCOIN is wholly digital and not tangible, it is impossible to have any physical deterioration.

Portability

The problem with gold and fiat currencies are the security risks, which include storage space and overall transportability. If you choose to have your savings close by, in your home or directly on you, this poses obvious risks such as personal robberies and home burglaries. The alternative for gold is to use a physical vault which can become costly, impractical and time inefficient. As for fiat currencies, the alternative is typically storing your funds in a bank, and you now know the disasters that arise from leaving your money in centralised custody.

Travelling is fun, right? So what happens if you want to live abroad for a period of time, or even move on a more permanent basis? Bringing your gold bullion bars abroad is completely impractical and in most cases illegal, depending on the quantity. This also applies to physical fiat currencies, as this will most likely arouse suspicion and possible criminal implications depending on the quantity. It seems the only logical action to take is to leave your gold bullion bars behind, with no accessibility and with complete faith and trust in whoever is storing your gold. Good luck with that!

BITCOIN on the other hand is as simple as clicking a few buttons, additionally there isn't a minimum or maximum quantity you're permitted to take on your journey. Whether it is $1 or $100 million, the price to send and receive between wallets is negligible compared to moving large sums of gold across borders. With BITCOIN, this is not necessary, you just need to take your wallet or pocket-size cold storage device around the world with you!

Escaping Tyranny And Genocide: Nazi Germany

Here's a raw perspective on the value BITCOIN offers and why I consider it humanitarian money. When people flee tyrannical regimes, they have to leave their country with the clothes on their backs. They cannot take their local currency since it will be worthless in their migrating country. Furthermore, taking valuable possessions such as cars, paintings and jewellery is too difficult to carry and potentially dangerous, attracting the wrong attention. The ultimate choice for these people and their families is to remain living under persecution or migrate into poverty. BITCOIN's unique technology solves this exact problem as it empowers you to carry your wealth around the world with you and become truly sovereign.

For example, during the Holocaust, Nazi Germany stole the valuable possessions of Jewish people, including the gold in their teeth. To counter these atrocities, Jews fleeing Europe wrapped their gold in bread and swallowed it, just to ensure they had valuables in their new respective migrant countries. This tyrannical dehumanisation would not be possible in a world where BITCOIN has mass adoption. Remember, BITCOIN is cryptographically locked away and is therefore non-confiscatable. You can flee tyranny and genocide with the keys in your head. BITCOIN really is humanitarian money.

Divisibility

Typically when investing money into the stock market you may come across share prices of $400,000, like Berkshire Hathaway. This makes it difficult for the average person to invest and build wealth. However, BITCOIN can be divided into eight decimal places, making 100 million "satoshis" equate to one entire BITCOIN. This structure is similar to fiat currencies, where 100 cents equates to one Dollar; however, evidently nowhere near as divisible or practical. Therefore, despite BITCOIN trading at a high entry point of $50,000, divisibility enables the average person the opportunity to have "skin in the game" by buying as little as five Dollars. So spread the word and tell all your friends and family, BITCOIN is for everyone and not just an exclusive investment for the elite and rich.

The BITCOIN community envisages a world of "hyperbitcoinisation" where goods and services are denominated in BITCOIN and satoshis. To achieve this level of commercial mass adoption, divisibility is imperative. For example, how can you buy a loaf of bread with one BITCOIN? Well, you can but that's a

$50,000 loaf of bread. Therefore, as the value of BITCOIN increases so does the need for satoshis to enable all goods and services to be traded at a scalable level.

Uniformity

This refers to the physical characteristics of money remaining consistent. For example, all ten-dollar bills look the same and are accepted as the same numerical value to eliminate any confusion and create uniformity. Nevertheless, every so often central banks rebrand the physical appearance of a currency, disrupting the uniformity and triggering an urgent recall. The people have a limited period of time to exchange the soon to be invalid money for the newly accepted version. Unfortunately, in most cases millions of Dollars are left unchanged and worthless, sitting on people's shelves and bedside drawers.

BITCOIN smashes uniformity out of the park and will never encounter this problem. Fundamentally, BITCOIN does not possess any physical branding and is simply made up of math and code as a digital currency.

Fungibility

The fungibility of money is the foundation of a functioning society and refers to everyone having the same measure of numerical value. Fiat currencies are the most common example of this; the Dollar in my pocket is equal to and therefore directly interchangeable with the Dollar in your pocket. To explain this further, collectable items such as paintings and sports cards may not be fungible with their exact copy, because often their value is reliant on the condition, history and scarcity status. Could you imagine trying to buy your daily necessities in a society where everyone's money is valued differently? The economy would be in complete shambles, and would be nearly impossible to buy and sell goods with one another.

Often the durability of fiat currencies will impact its fungibility. For example, if you give me ten one-pound coins in exchange for a torn ten-pound note, you may believe the value is different and might choose to refuse it. However, one BITCOIN will always be directly interchangeable with another BITCOIN, fulfilling the fungibility criteria.

In spite of this, it's important I deliver an intellectually honest and comprehensive insight into BITCOIN, after all this is Undressing Bitcoin where nothing is off-limits. There is a debate in which BITCOIN is considered to be not entirely fungible for one significant reason. During the early years of BITCOIN, the currency was often used to conceal the purchase of illegal items such as drugs and weapons. This was undertaken on a clandestine dark web known as Silk Road.

Subsequently, the transactional history of the early minted BITCOINs can be traced back to criminal activities, due to the transparency and immutability of the blockchain. With this information available, a small number of people may wish to pay a higher premium for newly minted BITCOIN, in order to avoid absolute association with past illicit activities. In reality, this is not something to be concerned about, as I have yet to meet someone that has made this request, however, it's important that you understand the full landscape.

Acceptability

Acceptability as a monetary concept literally refers to whether your money will be accepted as a medium of exchange to trade goods and services. For example in today's world, imagine attempting to buy high street clothes with gold. As I write this book, BITCOIN has only been around for a nominal 12 years. Therefore, it's unrealistic to expect mass adoption and widespread acceptability. However, if we go by the current rate of adoption, widespread acceptability is inevitable, especially given the extraordinary events I'm about to discuss that took place in 2021.

On June 9th 2021, El Salvador became the first country in the world to pass a law that recognises BITCOIN as legal tender. As of now, it is possible for every single person in the country to trade goods and services entirely in BITCOIN! Just let that sink in for a second. That's an entire country accepting BITCOIN as payment. If that's not the path to mass adoption I don't know what is…

This move is completely unprecedented and sent shockwaves throughout the entire cryptocurrency community and Latin America. Following the news, countries including Mexico, Argentina, Brazil, and Paraguay all had very interesting reactions on social media, such as posting the bullish laser eye BITCOIN meme. I'll leave you to interpret that as you wish.

Remember the hyperinflation in Venezuela and the terrible results that came from it? Well, these Latin American countries face similar issues. Shortly after the El Salvador announcement, I tweeted:

"The humanitarian case for bitcoin is becoming more obvious every day. Forget digital gold, THIS is the most important narrative we should be teaching the world."

One of the many responses that really moved me was the following:

"My family are from Latin America. You know how horrible it was to send money to my family before I discovered Bitcoin?"

This person went on to express extreme dissatisfaction with the current method of sending money internationally through Western Union, due to the high fees and long delays. However, in this new technology-driven world with BITCOIN at the forefront, international transfers are more efficient and inexpensive. This is especially relevant and beneficial to those sending and receiving money in less economically developed countries.

Although El Salvador is the first country to legalise BITCOIN nationwide, it's still possible to spend your BITCOIN on goods and services around the world. Every day another payment provider shifts into the cryptocurrency space, becoming an intermediary between customers and merchants to facilitate BITCOIN payments. An excellent example of a mainstream corporation facilitating BITCOIN payments is PayPal. The payment provider made the innovative decision to allow customers to buy and sell crypto on its platform. Therefore, users now have the capacity to buy goods and services with BITCOIN, from PayPal's 26 million online merchants. Another winning example is Visa's integration with Crypto.com, which allows users to top up their visa card with

BITCOIN and spend on everyday items. So practically speaking, you could buy your morning coffee with BITCOIN. Forget the path to mass adoption, it sounds like it has already arrived!

If you can take one thing from this chapter, it should be that BITCOIN is inherently borderless, indiscriminate and autonomous. As a currency, it does not serve a specific country, skin colour, religion or ethnicity; it "belongs" to the blockchain and is run by the people and for the people.

CHAPTER 5

Undressing BITCOIN Myths

It's likely when you first heard of BITCOIN, from that nerdy guy living in his mum's basement, or in my case, a druggie friend when I was 17, you only thought negative things. If only at the time you had someone to decipher these concerns for you, perhaps you would be a millionaire by now... Too bad, I was busy then, but I'm free now. So here it is in a clear and direct way.

These are the three biggest myths concealing the reality of BITCOIN:

1. BITCOIN is for criminals
2. BITCOIN is a scam
3. BITCOIN is bad for the environment

Bitcoin For Criminals

One of the oldest myths out there is that BITCOIN is used by criminals and helps facilitate illicit activities. People have negative connotations largely due to BITCOIN's usage back in the early days. BITCOIN was often used as the medium of exchange on the dark web, such as Silk Road, which was famously shut down by the FBI in 2013. It's important to distinguish that BITCOIN did not become the primary currency for criminal activity because of its underlying technology. However, during this time period, BITCOIN was new and unheard of, which meant authorities had little comprehension of how to regulate and trace it. The lack of BITCOIN understanding from authorities left room for a subculture to emerge, which criminals naturally gravitated towards, taking full advantage of this new and unheard-of means of exchange.

In stark contrast, BITCOIN is in fact an unintelligent choice to conduct criminal activities with. Despite the anonymity of wallet addresses, the blockchain technology that BITCOIN is built on empowers all transactions to be entirely traceable, transparent and immutable. Authorities literally have the ability to follow a criminal trail of breadcrumbs, all the way to the original source, leaving an irreversible mark. Consequently transacting in BITCOIN for illicit purposes is almost identical to pleading guilty and exposing all known accomplices, how stupid can you get?

In today's reality, the world's understanding of BITCOIN has developed to an extent where criminals are in fact moving away from BITCOIN as their primary choice of currency. A study by the University of Oxford, conducted back in 2017, found that 44% of all BITCOIN transactions were associated with criminal activity. However, only 2 years later, a report by Chainalysis showed that less than 1% of BITCOIN activity was criminal. This monumental decrease in illicit activity illustrates the shift in criminal sentiment, and that only a fool would continue to undertake criminal activities using BITCOIN.

How ironic is this: data from the United Nations shows between 2 to 5% of global GDP, that's 8 hundred billion to 2 trillion U.S. Dollars, is in fact laundered through fiat currencies. I personally think it's now crystal clear which is the preferred method for criminals, don't you?

Tax Evasion And Tax Avoidance

Another common myth surrounding BITCOIN is its ability to enable tax evasion and tax avoidance on large scales. In reality, BITCOIN cannot be laundered or concealed any more than fiat currencies, as the same tax preventions and measures apply to all forms of assets and income. For example, an employee earning a salary solely in BITCOIN or any other cryptocurrency will have their total gross income legally recorded on the company's accounts. Therefore, despite your salary potentially going into an anonymous wallet, the tax authorities have full knowledge of how much you earn and owe the tax authorities.

For all entrepreneurial business people, such as sole traders and business owners, once again just like fiat currency, it is entirely your responsibility to honestly disclose your crypto income. Furthermore, all the "crypto ballers" that want to flex their millions on luxurious cars, watches and a jet-set lifestyle, will require fiat currency to make these extravagant purchases. Therefore, when trading crypto for fiat on an exchange, the company or individual will encounter KYC due diligence, ultimately identifying them with their undeclared income. In a highly unlikely scenario whereby the tax authorities haven't caught their undeclared income, the extravagant spending on luxurious items will inevitably trigger a serious tax enquiry.

I personally find it interesting that people associate BITCOIN with criminal activity, when in fact physical cash is one of the biggest conduits for tax evasion and other illicit activities. Exchanging physical cash for goods and services is the most efficient way to remain anonymous, leaving tax authorities none the wiser. Some of the biggest culprits of this include Pablo Escobar, modern cartels and cash businesses.

Is BITCOIN A Scam?

In recent times we've seen major players such as MicroStrategy and Elon Musk's Tesla deploy billions of dollars into BITCOIN. Yet despite these credible industry names, there are still rumours floating around that BITCOIN is a scam and more specifically, a Ponzi scheme.

So what is a Ponzi scheme?

Briefly speaking, a Ponzi scheme is a type of fraud where a company attracts investors to deposit money in trust, while investors are led to believe there's a strategic investment plan. However, the original investors' capital is never invested but rather spent by the company on luxurious unrelated items. Here comes the fraud: in order to show and pay a return to the original investors, the company entices new investors and fraudulently uses these funds to pay back the original investors. An example of a notorious case is Bernie Madoff, who literally "made off" with everyone's money.

Is BITCOIN a Ponzi scheme?

Unlike a Ponzi scheme, Bitcoin is a decentralised network where investors have full autonomy over their funds, making it a "trustless" system. Ultimately due to its core values, it is impossible for Bernie Madoff and other crooks to buy Ferraris and mansions with your BITCOIN. As the network has no central authority, your funds were never in their crooked custody in the first instance, but rather securely locked away on the blockchain. Furthermore, BITCOIN serves an actual purpose with real utility, whether that be a store of value (digital gold) or a medium of exchange. On the other hand, Ponzi schemes are not providing any economic value to their investors or the system as a whole. Instead, the company owner(s) just spends your money and flexes until their time is up.

In the highly unlikely event all BITCOIN investors sold and withdrew their money simultaneously, the market price would massively decrease, however, the network would continue to survive and operate as usual. Ponzi schemes, on the other hand, would cease to exist, which is exactly what happened in the case of Bernie Madoff.

The Truth About BITCOIN's Carbon Footprint

One of the hottest topics passionately and aggressively debated by everyone, from the mainstream media to anonymous social media accounts and back to Elon Musk, is whether BITCOIN has a large negative impact on the environment. When discussing BITCOIN's energy consumption and its impact on the environment we must remain intellectually honest. You will often hear the claim, "the Bitcoin network is green". However, I prefer to regard the network as a "greener" alternative to the current financial system. Realistically speaking, Bitcoin is indeed a network that consumes large amounts of energy, there's no doubt about it. Ultimately the point is, can you tell me an industry as value-returning as BITCOIN which does not consume large amounts of energy?

BITCOIN continues to be at the centre of the firing line, as its energy consumption is criticised for what I regard as frivolous and feeble-minded reasons. Its youth, disruptive technology and fast- growing popularity pose an enormous threat to the current financial system. This is why it's no surprise; the establishment cowardly attacks what they don't understand and what they fear.

For example, if the energy consumption concerns are genuine, why is nobody talking about Christmas lights? Yes, you read that correctly. Typically Christmas lights in the U.S. consume 6.63 billion kilowatt-hours of electricity each year, for a trivial purpose with no real value other than aesthetic entertainment. To put this into perspective, according to phys.org, this sum is greater than the annual national energy consumption of developing nations, including El Salvador and Ethiopia.

Why am I constantly hearing gold and fiat currency propaganda when in reality nobody is paying anywhere near as much attention to the astronomical carbon footprint left behind from these traditional systems? Bitcoin Magazine amalgamated data from several credible sources including Dell and the Cambridge Bitcoin Electricity Consumption Index, and the results are fascinating...

The entire gold industry, which includes mining, refining and recycling, has an approximate total CO_2 output of 144 million tonnes! Its guilty partner in crime, the entire traditional banking system which includes the production of physical currency, bank branches and ATMs, has an approximate total CO_2 output of a whopping 408 million tonnes! Collectively this is an unimaginable and gigantic total of over half a billion tonnes of CO_2, polluting God's green earth.

Now for the moment you have all been waiting for: Bitcoin's CO_2 output as of 2021 is around a much more respectable 70 million tonnes. Additionally, Bitcoin's output is not directly correlated to the number of transactions on the network. Subsequently, as the number of users increases, the system does not necessarily require more energy, which is in complete contrast to the traditional financial system.

Where are the clickbait headlines and climate change activists and why is no one talking about the above?

Can You Power A Bank Branch In England With The Volcanoes In El Salvador?

No... But you can certainly power BITCOIN with it, keep reading!

In spite of BITCOIN winning in all of the above categories, the most innovative solution to growing environmental concerns is through something I like to call "energy arbitrage". Essentially, the decentralised network allows BITCOIN mining to be geographically independent, enabling mining from anywhere around the world. This is unique to BITCOIN and incentivises miners to source the most inexpensive energy, as energy prices are not globally fungible due to supply and demand. This is the first time we are witnessing the decentralisation of energy production, and where the term "energy arbitrage" comes into play.

For example, renewable power plants are built with the foresight to serve the growing energy demands of the future and not the current demands of the present. Consequently, large amounts of energy generated from renewable power plants are constantly wasted, therefore making the energy unexploited and inexpensive. This is because renewable energy, such as solar energy, cannot be switched off for obvious reasons. Ultimately, the financial cost and future return on investment can take decades to recuperate. This opens up a logical opportunity for miners to swoop in and harness all the unused and inexpensive energy. With this logic, miners are incentivised to seek out cheaper energy opportunities from wasted resources, making the Bitcoin network a greener solution.

To be crystal clear about the actuality of BITCOIN's greener energy, the Cambridge Centre for Alternative Finance (CCAF) estimated as of 2018, that 39% of BITCOIN mining is powered by renewable energy such as hydroelectric. This number will only increase in time with more mining farms gravitating towards this direction, given the inexpensive mining opportunities all around the world.

For example, just three years later we are already seeing this swift increase in renewable energy. In 2021 El Salvador's President announced plans to build a BITCOIN mining facility utilising geothermal energy from the country's volcanoes. This would be 100% renewable energy with zero CO_2 emissions! Just another example in which BITCOIN naturally gravitates towards green energy and innovates in new ideas. And, just as the title reads, the era of powering a monetary system from volcanoes begins...

Despite everything mentioned above and keeping true to my promise of intellectual honesty, BITCOIN mining is not perfect and building these mining facilities will always require a degree of energy. However, as Satoshi Nakomoto once said before he or they disappeared, and I paraphrase:

BITCOIN mining is a "net positive for the environment... Not mining bitcoin would be a net waste... Gold mining is a waste, but that waste is far less than the utility of having gold available".

Essentially, this quote inspires the question, is BITCOIN really worth it? When considering its value, from individual autonomy and decentralisation to the humanitarian benefits and the net positivity for the environment, what do you think?

CHAPTER 6

Seeking The "OG" BITCOIN

A s you navigate through this new world of internet money, you might come across numerous cryptocurrencies that have BITCOIN in their names. Nevertheless, it's extremely important to realise there is only one true Bitcoin network, and therefore only one BITCOIN. The most popular cryptocurrencies that include BITCOIN in their names are networks that have completed a process known as a "hard fork". This refers to a division of ideas within the BITCOIN community, where a large group advocates for new rules on the network. The division of ideas ignites large debate and eventually leads to a fork in the road, resulting in the emergence of an entirely new blockchain and coin. As hard forks derive from the "OG" BITCOIN, the coins often retain many of the same properties and characteristics, whilst also owning new network rules. An important point to remember is these new coins have absolutely no fungibility with the "OG" BITCOIN.

Over the years BITCOIN has received tremendous amounts of criticism for its scalability issues, which refers to its slow and expensive transactions, especially during times of high volume. Since BITCOIN was created to be the alternative system, delayed transactions and expensive network fees are completely illogical. For example, imagine buying a cup of coffee with BITCOIN and the transaction fee being greater than the coffee itself. With this reality, parts of the community decided to change the rules of the network, in order to fulfil the original objective. The two most well- known BITCOIN forks are Bitcoin Cash (BCH) created in 2017, and Bitcoin SV (BSV) created in 2018.

However, the network changes did not come without resistance from the community as many believed it meant compromising part of BITCOIN's core values. In order to improve the transaction speed and fees, the block size was increased from 1MB to 32MB. The idea being the greater the block size, the more transactions it can accommodate, resulting in faster confirmation times and inexpensive fees. Subsequently solving the scalability problem and creating an entirely new blockchain and coin known as Bitcoin Cash.

But the fork in the road did not stop there, once again further division arose amongst the different factions, and more scalability was protested. With this being the case, Bitcoin Cash underwent its own unique hard fork, and thus Bitcoin SV was born. One of the core distinctions between Bitcoin Cash and Bitcoin SV is the block sizes, which saw a monumental increase from 32MB to 128MB, and at one point confirming a block of 638MB in 2021!

Unfortunately, as the saying prevails, you cannot have your cake and eat it. The Bitcoin Cash and Bitcoin SV sectors might have achieved their respective outcomes, nevertheless, this did not come without major backlash. BITCOIN maximalists believe blockchain scalability is possible only if you're willing to pay the price and sacrifice one of BITCOIN's principal philosophies, DECENTRALISATION. Consequently, this core value could not be compromised, and therefore new blockchains were established with the Bitcoin network remaining unchanged. Ultimately, decentralisation empowers BITCOIN to be the most secure and reliable computer network in the world. It's commonly argued that increasing block sizes exposes the network to cyber hackers and greater centralisation of miners.

Wrapped BITCOIN

Unlike the above three coins, there is an entirely separate network that hosts a token by the name of Wrapped BITCOIN (WBTC). This token serves an entirely different purpose and is an asset that represents BITCOIN on the Ethereum network. Before we begin to understand its existence, we must briefly understand the Ethereum network.

Ethereum is a decentralised blockchain that enables "smart contract" functionality, founded in July 2015 by the computer programmer Vitalik Buterin. The native cryptocurrency of the Ethereum network is Ether (ETH). Ethereum at the time of writing this book has become the second-largest cryptocurrency after the "OG" king, BITCOIN. In the same way BITCOIN is known as the king of cryptocurrencies, ETH is widely considered the king of altcoins.

Altcoins are the other alternative cryptocurrencies that are not BITCOIN. At the time of writing, there are roughly over 8,000 different coins.

For the purpose of keeping this book Undressing Bitcoin and not Undressing Ethereum, I'm going to summarise a key difference between the two networks. A friend once explained to me that Bitcoin is digital gold, whereas Ethereum is quite like the internet, but superior in many ways. BITCOIN is a store of value and a long- term hedge against inflation. Ethereum is a programmable network that enables multi-varied applications from decentralised finance to decentralised games and social media platforms.

Launched in January 2019, Wrapped BITCOIN provides the necessary representation for BITCOIN holders to access the Ethereum network, as the respective blockchains are not interoperable. In order to wrap your BITCOIN into what is known as an ERC20 token, you must deposit your BITCOIN with the custodian, BitGo Trust. In turn, the custodian provides you with your Wrapped BITCOIN, enabling full access to explore the Ethereum network.

WBTC is directly backed 1 to 1 with BITCOIN, and therefore the price charts should appear almost identical. Keeping in line with the ethos of transparency and verifiability, the amount of WBTC in circulation has been made public to ensure it is backed accurately and securely. The crucial point is BITCOIN holders do not want to sell their BITCOIN, therefore "wrapping" allows them full access to the new world of decentralised finance while also maintaining their exposure to the greatest appreciating asset of the decade. If the world of decentralised finance continues to grow as expected, so will the popularity of wrapping coins.

CHAPTER 7

Undressing Bitcoin's Challenges

There's no denying one of BITCOIN's biggest challenges so far is the scalability issue, which refers to delayed transaction times and high fees. This obviously is not ideal when seeking to replace the traditional system. In order for BITCOIN to fulfil its original vision, the network must be able to process vast amounts of transactions on a global scale. To put this into perspective, the payment network Visa processes on average 4,000 transactions per second and has the capability to scale up to 64,000 transactions per second. On the other hand, Bitcoin can process a much smaller seven transactions per second, so Bitcoin developers came up with their own solution, which doesn't require an entirely new and separate blockchain or coin.

This new and innovative solution is called the Lightning network and was first proposed by developers in 2015. The Lightning network is a layer two network that runs directly on top of the original Bitcoin network, relying on the base layer for security and immutability. Since Lightning is a secondary network and not a blockchain, it does not have its own coin, but rather has the sole purpose of facilitating faster and inexpensive BITCOIN transactions.

How Does The Lightning Network Operate?

The layer 2 network allows two parties to establish a payments channel between them, by depositing funds to a multi-signature wallet, which requires both parties' authorisation, hence multi- signature. This is known as the funding transaction and is recorded and secured on the Bitcoin base layer. Both parties on either side of the channel have their own respective balance based on the initial funding. For example, Layah and Gideon open up a channel, Layah deposits £50 and Gideon deposits £100, the total balance of the multi-signature wallet is now £150. Layah and Gideon can then send and receive funds between themselves, up to the total amount initially deposited, £150. Think of this as a running tab between the two parties on the Lightning network, where transactions are almost instant and feeless because they are not processed on the Bitcoin base layer.

When Layah sends money to Gideon, she signs what is known as a "commitment transaction" which is also countersigned by the receiver, Gideon. At this point, the transaction is finalised and the funds have transferred ownership from Layah to Gideon. Furthermore, the counter signature is a vital security mechanism that ensures neither party sends or receives funds from the multi- signature wallet without the other person's permission. If either party decides they want to exit the channel, the final balance is recorded onto the Bitcoin base layer. In the event Layah disappears, a built-in mechanism ensures Gideon's funds can still be released, irrespective of Layah's counter signature.

Here's where it gets interesting, to transact with the rest of the world in BITCOIN through this new, speedy and inexpensive network, there is no need to establish multiple payment channels.

To give you some perspective, this is similar to connecting a computer or mobile phone to an internet provider, which in return gives you access to the world wide web. The Lightning network was built with the purpose of scaling Bitcoin's user base globally, in order to make transactions more efficient and inexpensive for everyday use.

However, the Lightning network has not come without major criticism, and I want to be as unbiased as possible and share this critique for your consideration. At the time of writing this book, Lightning has not received widespread adoption within the community, largely due to its unfriendly user experience and complex functionality. Furthermore, the community's obvious dissatisfaction with this solution is evident, from the Bitcoin Cash and Bitcoin SV forks established two to three years after the Lightning network. However, like all new and emerging technologies, I'm certain the user experience will improve and more people will be willing to migrate to the network.

In addition to educating my online and wider community about BITCOIN, I have also had the fortune and pleasure of interviewing crypto thought leaders and investors on my weekly podcast. So I would like to share a thought-provoking interpretation of BITCOIN's purpose that one of my guests presented to me. In May 2020, I interviewed Mark Yusko who is the founder and CEO of the investment management firm Morgan Creek Capital Management. We discussed how BITCOIN critics often compare BITCOIN to steam trains, MySpace, and to Nokia mobile phones. The critics admit Bitcoin was the technology that sparked the revolution, however, argue the scalability concerns leave room for future iterations and more efficient cryptocurrencies.

Nevertheless, despite this critique and general sentiment, Mark Yusko gave me an extremely insightful perspective which explained Satoshi Nakomoto prioritised security over efficiency. I personally believe this is one of the truest and most accurate statements I have ever heard when discussing BITCOIN's purpose. When considering this statement further, you realise BITCOIN transactions might be slow and expensive from time to time, however, this is evidently the price you pay for the highest level of security, immutability and decentralisation in a network. Furthermore, with a little more time and patience, the Lightning network, or future layer two iterations, could solve the scalability concerns.

CHAPTER 8

The Future of BITCOIN

Rising BITCOIN Hostility

———•◦◇◦•———

The meteoric rise of BITCOIN and general cryptocurrencies in 2021 saw everyone from your family and friends all the way to major institutions like Goldman Sachs try to get a piece of the pie. Nevertheless, BITCOIN's rockstar-like rise and status inevitably caught the attention of regulators and the wider establishment.

For example, the UK regulator, the Financial Conduct Authority (FCA), is preparing an £11 million marketing campaign with the purpose of cautioning young British people about the risk of cryptocurrencies. Furthermore, at the time of writing the FCA has also cracked down on cryptocurrency exchanges in the UK, resulting in Barclays and NatWest customers unable to send payments to and from the Binance exchange. In both cases the FCA and UK banks justify these aggressive regulatory decisions with the typical response we've heard time and time again: "We're doing this to protect you".

I find this extremely ironic as the gambling industry and more specifically online casinos can be a far more dangerous and addictive entrapment. However, the FCA has put nowhere near as much time and resources into "protecting the people" from the serious repercussions of addictive online gambling. Moreover, a more productive and viable use of the £11 million would be investing this money into the school curriculum, teaching young people financial literacy. This will ensure the future generation grows up with a sound comprehension of how to create long-lasting wealth and avoid suffocating debt, which in many cases ends up ruining lives.

Can BITCOIN Be Banned?

To answer this question I'm going to give you another example of aggressive hostility towards BITCOIN, which hopefully will give you the answer. Enter, CHINA. In mid-2021, China became so malevolent towards BITCOIN that mining operations in several provinces were coerced into shutting down. Naturally, the price of BITCOIN fell in response to the news, however, within less than a week, two of the largest BITCOIN mining companies relocated their operations to Kazakhstan. Ultimately, BITCOIN does not need China or any specific country or region for that matter. The decentralised network will continue to operate despite any forms of crypto sanctions. In fact, China's malevolence has only empowered BITCOIN's decentralisation to a higher extent, as mining operations are now no longer concentrated in one country, but rather sparsely dispersed across the globe.

Nigeria is another classic example of government hostility towards BITCOIN, which in turn only ends up becoming a net positive for the network. Not many people are aware, but

Nigeria is the second-largest BITCOIN market after the U.S., due to the Central Bank of Nigeria (CBN) continuously devaluing the local currency, the Naira.

Here are a few of the economic restrictions in Nigeria:

- **$100 spending cap a month on international websites**
- **An average inflation rate of 16% per annum**
- **Extortionate fees to send money home from overseas work**
- **Prohibited payment websites such as PayPal to get paid from overseas work**
- **Blocked bank accounts for taking part in protests against government actions**
- **Naira debit cards cannot be used abroad to withdraw Dollars, Euros or Pounds**

With these restrictions on freedom, it's no surprise Nigeria has become the second-largest BITCOIN market in the world. Continuing with this tyrannical theme, in February 2021 the Central Bank of Nigeria warned other banks and financial institutions, "facilitating payments for cryptocurrency exchanges is prohibited". Once again like China, these crypto sanctions backfired, skyrocketing BITCOIN to trade at a premium of 60% ($80,000) on the Luno exchange. Despite the ban, Nigerians were willing to pay this premium, because they understood the value that BITCOIN offers when it comes to protecting their wealth. Thanks largely to the CBN, further BITCOIN magic happened! Peer-to-peer BITCOIN trading shot up by 27% increasing the "mass adoption" of BITCOIN.

One of the beauties in BITCOIN seems to be the more a government utilises its resources to eradicate it, the more Satoshi Nakomoto's vision of a decentralised store of value is being fulfilled. In other words, the more the establishment attacks BITCOIN, the stronger BITCOIN becomes. It might sound strange but this seems to be the physical laws of cause and effect coming into fruition.

Why Governments Want To Ban BITCOIN

With governments all around the world acting like mafia bosses, dictating what we can and can't do with our hard-earned money, it begs the question, what is so unique and perhaps even threatening about BITCOIN? In my opinion, because BITCOIN triggered such an enormous negative reaction from authorities around the world, there must be more to the story than regulators trying to "regulate".

I believe BITCOIN threatens the power and control the current establishment possesses over the average person, and this threat is only increasing as technology and time advances. The establishment refers to international governments around the world, and intergovernmental organisations such as the United Nations, European Union, International Monetary Fund and the World Bank. These organisations realise BITCOIN provides the world with an opportunity to "opt-out" of an obsolete and declining system backed by debt. You see, in order for the traditional system to survive, the establishment requires as a prerequisite your investment of time, money and energy. And just like a vampire, the establishment will drain you of your resources and livelihoods to keep the public at large trapped in an enslavement machine.

Based on all the above examples of BITCOIN surpassing fiat currency in all capacities, the world is waking up and realising BITCOIN is the solution to the fiat currency problem. One of the biggest players desperate to capitalise on this revolutionary technology, believe it or not, is your very own trusted and local government. DO NOT BE FOOLED, your government will encourage and persuade you to shift your money into their new "trusted" Central Bank Digital Currency, otherwise known as CBDCs.

Essentially, CBDCs are no different to fiat currencies, and in fact are a digital version of the Dollar, Pound and Euro. To be crystal clear, CBDCs will most likely use blockchain technology, HOWEVER, the network will be entirely centralised by the government, defeating the very purpose of BITCOIN. The CBDC is merely the new digital currency for the central bank, controlled by exactly the same mindless people. These bureaucratic vampires will implement exactly the same monetary and fiscal policies, continuing to devalue your money and create nothing but debt and poverty. You will hear buzzwords and sound bites such as "Our digital currency is government-backed... Our digital currency is better for the environment". DO NOT BELIEVE this propaganda for one second!

The CBDC is a far more efficient enslavement machine since the entire system will be digitised. For example, remaining consistent with Joe Biden's bright ideas like pumping $1.9 trillion into the economy, with CBDCs this will be done more efficiently. Moreover, as blockchain technology is entirely transparent, the government will have full access to all your transactions in a more efficient capacity, eliminating any privacy you thought you had left. To conclude this topic, stay away from CBDCs at all costs, you're better off keeping your paper fiat currency, as it's less of a dangerous enslavement machine.

In conclusion, BITCOIN was created to replace the traditional financial system, providing us with a currency that is borderless, humanitarian and fully decentralised. Furthermore, BITCOIN goes far deeper than making a "quick buck" on a rising asset, but rather having the choice to no longer be a slave to the establishment. BITCOIN is money that works for you, rather than against you, and whether BITCOIN can truly scale and replace the traditional financial system, only time will tell.

From my experience, being part of the BITCOIN and cryptocurrency community has been the greatest experience. From meeting other free-minded individuals to a feeling of having a kind of immunity from government and central bank corruption. No matter how much money they print, and regardless of the development of CBDCs, knowing that I am sovereign over my wealth is truly an empowering feeling.

ABOUT THE AUTHOR

Layah has dedicated the last 3 years of her career since 2018 to analysing and reporting on the cryptocurrency industry. She is a long-term bitcoin holder who chooses to receive her entire income solely in bitcoin.

After working abroad for Malta's leading cryptocurrency news channel for one year, she decided to begin her entrepreneurial ventures in the world of cryptocurrency media. Layah is a real advocate for personal responsibility, individual empowerment and freedom, and this precise philosophy is what drives her work.

When she is not covering the markets and interviewing high-profile guests for her show, you might find her on a white beach somewhere exotic.

Printed in Great Britain
by Amazon